WHEELBARROW
—— PROFITS ——

HOW TO CREATE PASSIVE INCOME, BUILD WEALTH,
AND TAKE CONTROL OF YOUR DESTINY THROUGH
MULTIFAMILY REAL ESTATE INVESTING.

JAKE STENZIANO AND GINO BARBARO

CONTENTS

ABOUT THE AUTHORS

Most people think about a better life, no matter how good they have it. At the core of these hopes is usually something related to money. They picture themselves living more comfortably, not stressing over credit card bills, the mortgage, or student loan debts, maybe going on vacation and getting to spend more time with their families.

Financial freedom is what they're wishing for. Most people don't believe it's attainable on their own, but rather something that has to be handed to them by way of luck, or through an exclusive opportunity. They think wealth can't be earned in today's economy, that the fantasy of being comfortable or getting ahead is just that: a dream. And as far as luck goes, they may be at least partially right.

Gino Barbaro graduated from Fairfield University in 1992 with a degree in finance, and subsequently struggled to locate a job in the terrible economy. He was fortunate to locate employment with AIG, though it was only through a bit of lucky networking that he was able to do so. He worked in the reinsurance accounting department, and quickly realized that watching paint dry was more pleasurable than working in insurance. Gino's father owned a restaurant where Gino had worked since he was eight years old and he returned there, rather than languish in a cubicle.

Gino still runs the restaurant to this day, but he realized years ago that, while running the restaurant was a great job, it would not allow him to accumulate wealth. That dream of financial freedom was ever present, but it seemed like it would always be just out of reach.

In addition to the restaurant, Gino's parents had also owned a number of investment properties, something which intrigued him. Following their example, he purchased his first multifamily property in 2002. The property consisted of a three-family home with a detached garage and office. The home was next to the restaurant and he could use one of the garages to store supplies and merchandise for the restaurant. The problem was, he wasn't quite sure what to do next. He began studying, learning more about the real estate industry and waiting for the right opportunity to come around.

Meanwhile, Jake Stenziano was working in sales for a top three pharmaceutical and vaccine manufacturer. The job paid well enough, and helped he and his wife get by, but as with most jobs in that field it would never be enough for them to truly be comfortable. In trying to get ahead and make those dreams of financial freedom slightly more attainable, Jake pushed for a transfer from Westchester, New York to Tennessee, where the cost of living was lower.

At the same time, he knew that his career was far from secure no matter where he went. The pharmaceutical company he was working for had six layoffs in eight years, resulting in thousands of lost jobs. Feeling like it was only a matter of time before his number was called, Jake began thinking about how he might secure a future for himself where he wasn't at the mercy of a corporate axe.

The one solution that stuck out to him came from one of his clients, a doctor he met with frequently through work. The doctor told Jake that the secret to attaining wealth had nothing to do with finding a great job or getting lucky. The secret was in real estate. It was an attractive idea, but Jake knew nothing about the market. He began doing some research, and resolved to see if he could find property in Tennessee to begin his investment portfolio.

What he found was that, much as the cost of living was lower there, so too was the cost of investing in properties. What's more, he identified a potentially lucrative market that seemed virtually unnoticed by the investors in the area: multifamily properties. Jake realized that these were self-sustaining, in that they could literally pay for themselves, and that there would always be a need for these apartment and condo complexes. It seemed too good to be true. He was moving someplace where he could live more comfortably and, potentially, start experimenting in real estate. Still, he wasn't totally comfortable with the idea of risking so much, and he too found himself debating what to do next.

Jake happened to frequent Gino's restaurant, as he was friends with Gino's brother Marco. On one of his last trips in before moving, he found himself at a table talking to Marco about his plans. It turned out that Marco had begun investing in real estate with Gino.

"Yeah, you should talk to my brother about that," Marco said. "He knows all about it."

Marco wasn't kidding. Gino had come a long way from a guy who didn't know what to do with his first multifamily property. When Gino and Jake sat down, they instantly found that they had the same goals. What's more, Jake had the perfect opportunity for them in multifamily real estate, and Gino knew the ins and outs of the business already. With Jake on location in Tennessee and Gino ready to share everything he knew about investing in real estate, they founded their partnership right there and never looked back.

Financial freedom isn't just a dream, it's something everyone can find for themselves. While you'll be responsible for finding the properties, within these pages you'll discover not only tips and best practices for uncovering that first opportunity, but a framework that will allow you to grow your portfolio from a single property to multiple revenue generating investments.

Today, what started out as a conversation between friends has exploded into a thriving real estate investment business that continues to grow in size and profitability. Jake and Gino both are now considered experts in real estate investment and have achieved, in just a few years, the sort of financial freedom they always wanted but weren't sure was possible. And while a certain amount of timing, coincidence, and luck brought them together, this book will be your partner, bringing that same luck, and years of experience, right to you every step of the way.

CHAPTER 1

INTRODUCTION

This book is going to show you how to become successful in multifamily real estate investing. The best advice we can give you is to negotiate everything and never give up. It's not going to be easy, especially in the beginning, but you'll notice that the process becomes routine the more involved you get and the longer you work at it.

When we started out, we had brokers trying to get us to sign exclusivity agreements. An exclusivity agreement gives the broker an exclusive right to represent us. This basically gives the broker a commission on any deal that you do, even if you found it yourself. This was all taking place before we even got the chance to look at properties. This was something that we never heard of and quickly realized that it was a self-serving proposition for the brokers to lock us in until they found something to sell us.

Fortunately, we declined this or we could have spent a lot of time in court. These same brokers soon became frustrated with us. You see, we were negotiating them down with creative financing, such as seller financing. We were trying to get lower down payments from the banks. If the asking price for the 25-50 unit complexes we looked at was more than we were willing to pay, we put in lower offers. We were doing everything we could think of to position ourselves with the best deals possible, to make every dollar stretch, but because we were just starting out these brokers thought we had zero credibility. Back then we didn't have any large multifamily units. Eventually one broker blew up at us. "You'll never do business in this town," he said angrily. "Things don't work like that down here!" This broker, and others like him, saw us as outsiders attempting to invade the Knoxville, TN real estate market, and they were determined to maintain their status quo.

We never worked with this self-proclaimed, "top salesman" after that. Side note – the next year, the broker that we have done the majority of our business with was awarded the Broker of the year award from CCIM's East TN chapter based on sales revenue.

We finally found a broker who aligned with our strategy, a partner we still have to this day, but after putting in offers for over a year we were at the point of giving up. We didn't feel like we were getting anywhere – no one would take our offers. What could we do? We had so much rejection. You can only get kicked down so many times. We decided to take a break and rethink our strategy, but at the time it was unclear if we would ever pick it up again.

About six months went by and we finally got the nerve to get back in the game. Shortly after we started looking at deals again we found one we knew we had to have. It was everything that we had been looking for: high vacancy rates and deferred maintenance. This was an ugly duckling property, but it had a ton of potential.

We decided to take one more stab at this multifamily thing. We ended up meeting with a broker and a banker at lunch. The banker said he wasn't interested in financing a class C type property with a lot of deferred maintenance. As we were walking down the street after lunch, Jake asked the broker, "Do you think they would be interested in seller financing for half the down payment?" We gave him a *very low* offer. The broker said, "Yeah, I think we can get that done."

We were shocked. Every other time we put in creative offers, the brokers just said we were nuts. But this broker said, "No, I think we can do it." A day later we were signing contracts at the table. We got a twenty-five unit mom-and-pop apartment complex and were off to the races. We were thrilled, but it left us scratching our heads. What the hell just happened?

It took us over two years to purchase our first property and it was hard. The number one thing that separated us from the thousands of investors who tried and failed was that we didn't quit. Well, at least not permanently. We took some time to reassess our strategy and we waited for the right property, but that was the single genius thing that we did. DON'T QUIT!

Once we bought our first property, our momentum and enthusiasm for the industry only continued to grow. We want you to succeed, and we want to help you get over the hurdles. Forget about having an extensive amount of money or experience – we didn't have either when we first started. What's important is how badly you want to own your first property and how much work you are willing to put in to get it.

Our ultimate goal was to make real estate a full time endeavor and continue to grow our portfolio, and years later we're still going strong. We wanted to have financial freedom and create passive income so we didn't have to settle for working nine-to-five jobs that didn't make us happy or provide us with the money we wanted. We're proof that anyone with passion, a plan, effort, and drive can achieve their goals. Are you ready to get started on the road to owning your first multifamily property?

Chapter 2

The Basics of Real Estate Investing

The number one reason that we started our partnership was to create wealth. We also wanted to transition our careers to investing fulltime. The remainder of the benefits in this chapter are simply icing on the cake.

Investing in real estate may seem difficult at first. It's major responsibility and it's not always a passive investment. There are also major barriers to entry. Many brokers won't take you seriously unless you have experience. These are just a few reasons why people never get started.

We view real estate not only as a way to produce wealth for ourselves, but also as the vehicle that will create generational wealth for our heirs. As multifamily owners, it's in your best interest to treat your tenants well. Not only are they paying your mortgage for you, but they give you a handsome return every month on your investment. Someday, you can pass that investment on from generation to generation. Hopefully, we'll have taught our kids enough about money, so that they will manage the asset properly.

The difference between passing on cash versus real estate is that the real estate will be paid off and have value on its own. It will also pay you every month, more than any interest rate would if you kept it in cash.

If you want to truly grow your wealth, you absolutely cannot rely on a single source of income."

There are three types of income. First and foremost, there's **earned income**. This is the type of income that most Americans earn, and is what you file with a W-2 when doing your taxes. Unfortunately, this type of income is taxed at the highest rate, and has very few deductions. Our goal is to turn our hard earned wages into passive income by investing in real estate and other passive streams of income.

The second type of income is called **portfolio income**. This type of income contains income from stocks, bonds, and mutual funds. This type of income is easier to manage than real estate, and therefore is more popular. Handing over the reins to a mutual fund company is an easy thing to do, and takes very little financial intelligence.

The third type of income is **passive income**. Passive income includes money from royalties, real estate earnings, and multi-level marketing. We feel that investors should diversify into owning a business, buying real estate, and owning paper assets. We find that passive income, earning money even if you aren't working, is the best way to make a living.

DANGERS OF RELYING ON EARNED INCOME

The majority of Americans rely on their nine to five job to pay their expenses. The biggest danger in relying on earned income is simple: if you can't work, you can't provide. If you ever become disabled and lose your job, that income dries up.

The other problem is that the more money you make as a W-2 employee, the more taxes you're going to pay. W-2 earners have very few tax deductions, meaning you won't be able to write off many expenses. That's why real estate is so attractive – anyone can set up a real estate endeavor as a business. This will afford you plenty of tax deductions. For example, if one of us buys a computer, we can get it deducted through our company. A W-2 earner would have to pay the full price and not receive a tax deduction. As a business owner, a lot of what you need can be deducted as a business expense. Gino's dad once told him "It's not what you make. It's what you keep that counts!"

The amount that wage earners pay in taxes is staggering. The average American works until the end of May, just to pay their taxes off. In other words, the first four or five months of their job, is earning money to give the government. It's just crazy, especially when you consider how risky it is to rely on someone else's decisions for your paycheck.

The middle class in America has been declining for decades. It's not uncommon to hear about major companies having massive layoffs and moving overseas. Real estate is our security. Because we invest in income producing assets, if we were to lose our other jobs we would still be okay. Our assets would still provide. Passive investments can give you much more protection, security, and freedom.

5 Benefits of Buying Real Estate Over Stocks

We wanted to build wealth, but neither of us viewed the stock market as our best option for that. Many have achieved wealth through the stock market, but we saw more promise in real estate for several reasons.

1. Control

The biggest problem with stocks is that you have no control. You can own the shares in a company, but unless you have a controlling stake you have zero control over the day-to-day operations. The CEO could make a stupid or irrational decision, the stock would plummet, and you have little to no influence over the management of the company. In real estate, you have complete control of the operations of your investment. Not only do you have no control over the investment, but also you have no control of the rapidly fluctuating market. Program trading accounts for roughly 70% of all stock trades through complex algorithms looking to make pennies per share. That's insanity. There's no long-term strategy there. Stock investment is a short-term strategy, where it just goes to the whim of the market, which can change in an instant. Real estate, on the other hand provides you with a long-term investment that you have direct control over.

2. Continuous Revenue

Stocks require you to sell the investment to cash out, which may trigger a capital gains tax. In real estate, there's no reason to kill the goose that lays the golden egg. Your tenants will pay your mortgage every month, and you will be generating cash flow. It's even possible to refinance the property to increase your return.

3. Flexible Pricing

Stocks have a defined market value at the time of purchase. There's no room for negotiation. With real estate, you can buy at a discount based on several factors. You can buy from motivated sellers such as a divorced couple, while a property is in probate, or from poor management. There are also options for creative pricing, such as seller financing, where the old owner agrees to finance a portion of the down payment. We will go over this in detail in the chapter, Finance Right.

4. Longer Time for Transaction

Real estate transactions are slower than stock transactions. With stocks, one push of the button, and the stock, or your investment capital, is gone; in real estate it can take a few months or even a year to complete a transaction. You have to really think about your strategy, and you have the time to make sure that you're making a wise decision.

This also provides time for you to do your due diligence. You can really go through the taxes and the operation. The owner had to turn over all these forms to you, and the lengthy transaction period gives you time to understand the investment. With a the stock, you're not privy to all that information. You have limited access to what you really will know about that company.

We think that's a positive. The average person doesn't have that kind of patience. Anyone can push a button and trade a stock. There's very little value in that. The market goes down, your want to sell that stock. Boom! It's sold on impulse. Two days later the stock runs up ten points and you're kicking yourself.

If prices go down in real estate, you can't sell because of the market. You're forced to hold on. Then three years later, prices go back up, and you're glad you kept that investment. In short, real estate has a built-in insulation from panic.

5. LEVERAGE

It's important to remember that you're leveraging other people's money. The tenants are paying down your monthly mortgage payments. This allows you to acquire assets and build equity with minimal personal risk. To minimize your risk further, you can use the bank's money to refinance or get creative with seller financing.

So, while $5,000 of stock only buys you $5,000, the same amount in a real estate down payment can buy you $40,000-$50,000 worth of real estate. Leverage is the most powerful thing when investing a real estate. If your asset goes up by 10%, your stock is worth $5,500, while in real estate it would be worth $44,000 if you had a property valued at $40,000. This would be an 80% gain out of one $5,000 investment! Leverage makes all the difference. We can control a highly leveraged multifamily apartment asset and force appreciation by repositioning an underperforming apartment complex. For those unfamiliar with repositioning, it's a process of cleaning up the property. It usually includes taking care of deferred maintenance and getting the rent up to market rates.

WHY PURCHASE MULTIFAMILY?

We find that within multifamily apartments there's less competition. There are fewer people out there doing multifamily deals than single-family deals, because they lack the mind-set and specialized knowledge. There's a nice niche where you get anywhere from 50 to 100 units, because it's usually too expensive for the average investor but is much too small for an institution to invest in, making **now** the time to invest. We've found several reasons why multifamily housing is much better for building wealth.

THE ECONOMY OF SCALE

We like being in control of our investment. When you have a large conglomerate controlling in it you have no idea what's really taking place on site. We prefer multifamily units to single families, because they're cheaper per unit. You may pay $50,000 or more per unit for a duplex, depending on your market, so you would make $50,000 per door. But we've found that, for a larger investment up front, you can get a 12-plex for $30,000 per unit. That's a 40% reduction in cost per unit! Because they're cheaper per unit you actually have a greater cash flow, as you'll rent it at a rate that is comparable to a single-family house. This is going to give you the ability to pay a team and professional management. With a larger complex, you'll also be able to take out a non-recourse loan. Non-recourse means that you won't be held personally liable in the unlikely event the investment fails. With a recourse loan, you'll have to pay back the full amount that you've borrowed.

These complexes are also less repair-intensive because they are central-ized into fewer buildings. You'll have less risk, because you have more tenants paying your monthly income. If you lose one of your tenants in a duplex, you're at 50% vacancy; if you lose one in an 8-plex, you'll still cover your bills every month. The main takeaway is this: More tenants, less risk.

This economy of scale also works in reverse, minimizing costs while increasing profits. For example, if you have six single-family houses, you're going to have six roofs to replace and repair, six lawns to mow, and six tenants spread out throughout the city. In an apartment complex, you have one property to maintain, but will still be able to collect rent from six or more tenants.

Having multi family units also protects you from inflation. Rents rise with inflation. When you have an apartment building, and inflation goes up 4-5%, rents tend to reflect that. This creates a hedge against inflation since you control the rent price.

WHY NOT COMMERCIAL REAL ESTATE?

There are plenty of people who purchase commercial real estate rather than apartment units. We think this is a much bigger risk than buying family homes. It won't be long before big-box stores like Best Buy or Home Depot will get rid of their commercial space or downsize. Going forward, people are going to be doing more online shopping. In 2014, online shopping accounted for 8% of total shopping in the United States and was growing at a 15% rate. As more people shop online, fewer people are going to visit the mall. That's just going to make turnaround more difficult if you invest in commercial real estate.

Besides losing big box stores, we're also noticing a distinct reduction in office space. As the middle class declines, there's going to be less of a need for people commuting to commercial office space.

More and more people work from their homes. Jobs are getting outsourced to India and to China. People are using virtual assistants in different countries. This creates a marked decline in office space. This also gives us a good reason to create a stable, steady investment that we control.

COST DEPRECIATION AND SEGREGATION

Depreciation can be defined as the recovery of your building acquisition cost through a tax deduction. This depreciation expense in your tax return does not require a current outlay of cash, as a general cost write off would. Tax laws allow for this non-cash deduction even while your asset actually *appreciates* in value. It's an excellent way to defer taxes on your profits, as your depreciation expense is possibly recaptured only when you sell the property. Just be sure to have your accountant calculate this non cash (phantom) expense.

When calculating depreciation, it's also important to look into cost seg-regation. What happens with cost segregation is that the depreciation deduction is accelerated.

The **cost segregation** is the process of identifying personal property, assets that are grouped with real property assets, and separating out personal assets for tax reporting purposes. For instance, when we buy an apartment building, assets such as hot water heaters, air conditioning units, and refrigerators are all segregated out of the building itself and then reclassified.

So, when you get to the point where you're buying larger multifamily buildings, it's important to look into cost segregation studies. This strategy will accelerate depreciation, and that will help you save on income taxes every year, especially if you file as a Limited Liability Company (LLC).

RISK ASSESSMENT

When purchasing your multifamily apartment, it's important to assess the risks involved. First, you should never buy a property with negative cash flow. This will send you directly to the poor house. You have to have a net positive when you purchase a property.

But how do you calculate risk? The difference between investing in real estate and an investment that is considered "risk free" is called the risk premium. It's actually rather simple calculation. Most investors use the 10-year Treasury bond as the barometer for risk-free investment. In 2014, the yield on the 10-year bond was about 2.2%. A cap rate is the rate of return on your real estate investment. If the cap rates in your market hover around 8 or 9%, and the 10-year bond is around 2%, then your risk premium is around 7%.

Each investor has to judge for themselves if it's worth their effort to invest in real estate if they're going to earn 7% above the 10-year bond rate. Remember, real estate has added risks along with tenants and toilets. We feel comfortable investing in real estate when the risk premium is at least 6%.

Back in 2006, savvy investors recognized the party was coming to an end. Cap rates had plummeted to around 5%, and the risk premium had shrunk significantly. The market subsequently went through a correction and the price dropped. Cap rates do have an inverse relationship with price, and the falling price lead to a higher cap rate. Once investors saw the risk premium rising again, it was their signal to return to the market.

AMORTIZATION

It's common in real estate to have fully **amortizing loans**. An amortizing loan is one in which the principle of the loan is paid down over the life of the loan, and each payment will consist of principle and interest. If the loan is not fully amortizing, and you lack the funds or assets to immediately make that payment, you might end up in default.

Amortizing your loan will help ensure that the expenses for your company will remain consistent, and that you won't have to pay off the remaining principle in one lump sum. We will explain how to finance your venture in more detail in "Finance Right."

VELOCITY OF MONEY

One reason why we like to invest in real estate and multi-families specifically is something called the **velocity of money**. This refers to how fast money passes from one holder to the next. Banks are a perfect example of "velocitizing" money. The faster the money moves, the greater the money supply you tap into, and the greater your dollar's earning power is. In our strategy, velocity of money works this way:

1. Invest in your asset.

2. Get your original investment back – this is where you refinance.

3. Keep control of the original asset that you have, which would be your multifamily property.

4. Move your refinanced investment in to a new asset or new property.

5. Repeat step number 2, refinance

6. Control that asset again

You're controlling assets and pulling money out by refinancing. That money is creating momentum. That's one way of building wealth extremely fast. Once you pull your money out, your rate of return becomes infinite, because you have no more capital invested in the deal. It was already taken out, and the risk that you have in your deal basically becomes nil because you will look to secure a **non-recourse loan**, so you're not going to be held personally liable for that debt. The only thing that is held liable in a non-recourse loan is the property itself, not your personal assets.

CAN I AFFORD THIS?

Learning how to invest in Multifamily properties can be challenging. But with America's shrinking middle class and unstable stock market, the question might not be "Can I afford to invest in Real Estate?" but rather, "Can I afford not to?" Our unique system will teach you how to identify the right property to invest in and how to buy right, finance right, and manage right. With our knowledge and expertise, you'll be generating stable, passive income for years to come.

CHAPTER 2 SUMMARY

Why Multifamily Real Estate?

1.) High cash on cash returns

2.) Equity through leverage (tenants are paying your mortgage)

3.) Assets that appreciate in value but depreciate from a taxation standpoint

Time for action

1.) What are you doing to decrease your dependency on earned income?

2.) How are you currently building wealth?

3.) How will owning multifamily change your current financial situation?

Check out www.jakeandgino.com for more wealth building tips

CHAPTER 3

THE PSYCHE OF A REAL ESTATE INVESTOR

Fear is one of the greatest obstacles keeping you from building wealth. We hear similar things from beginner investors all the time:

"I don't know where to start."

"I can't start investing right now because of my job."

"I don't have enough money."

"The time is not right."

Behind the excuse is usually a fear of change. People are afraid to take risks. They might lose money. They might fail.

As an investor, it's very important that you learn to become comfortable with fear. It's guaranteed to rear its ugly head at some point. We recommend getting an education to learn the ins and outs, the challenges and best practices, of the journey you are about to embark upon.

The only way to do this is by immersing yourself in real estate. When we started out, we had the same fears that most investors do, but we dealt with these fears by learning what was ahead and taking action. You must be rational and ask yourself, "What's the worst thing that could happen?" If you have the answer to this, you're ahead of the game.

Most people assume the worst without really knowing or understanding the reality of their situation.

At the end of the day, either you take action or fear wins. What's it going to be? Fear will not make you rich.

WHAT'S STOPPING YOU?

As Tony Robins says, "In order to make changes in your life, your should needs to become your must." Jake's company had 6 major layoffs in 8 years. As Jake saw thousands of people getting fired from their jobs, he knew it was time to make a change. Gino was burnt out at the restaurant and was sick of the rat race. He didn't see an opportunity to build wealth at the restaurant and needed to make a change.
We both started to attack the fears that were holding us back. We were more afraid of not acting and taking massive action than we were of failing. We both viewed staying in our current positions as failing. We didn't have all the knowledge that we needed in the beginning but we fully committed ourselves and it worked out.

Everyone has a specific fear to overcome. The most prominent one that we've encountered is fear of failure. When we first started in real estate, we were worried that we didn't understand the business well enough. It seemed like it would be all too easy to buy a property and stumble our way to failure, but we had to start somewhere.

It's important to keep in mind that failure is just success deferred. When we bought our first property, we did everything we could to verify what the broker, bank, and seller were telling us. The numbers had to match up perfectly before we went forward with the deal. This gave us the confidence to overcome our own fear of failure, and ensured our success.

STRESS

Stress is a code word for fear, and can be a major stumbling block. Fear has the power to deter even the most ambitious among us. Once you raise your consciousness to detect these feelings, you can meet them head on and choose to act.

Many people react to fear by engaging in excessive behavior such as overeating, smoking, or shopping. These actions break the pattern of stress, but the problem is still there. Learning how to overcome fear is tantamount to achieving success in any part of your life.

Your "should" has to become a "must" to effect lasting change. Think about the smoker who was told he has 6 months to live if he doesn't quit smoking. He's tried to quit for the last 30 years and nothing worked, but all of a sudden his "should" has transformed into a "must" in his mind.

Experiencing this urgency will push you forward, past stress and fear. Truly successful people show up every day and do their best, no matter what they're feeling. They set the goals they want to achieve, and let nothing stop them until they meet those expectations. Tenacity and commitment are what separates successful people from those who succumb to the pitfalls of anxiety and fear.

TIME TO COMMIT

Once you are able to push past these fears, it's time to commit. You must decide what you're going to achieve and how you are going to achieve it. When you get to this point, you will know it. This is when a certain type of awareness comes over you. Something inside of you just clicks and you know that no matter what, you're going to reach your goals. It's just a matter of time.

In fact, you can use your fears to drive that commitment. Fear of failure or mediocrity can push you out of your comfort zone. Our burning desire to be successful and to build wealth was worth the risk. For us, we just can't imagine what our lives would be like if we never gave real estate investment a shot.

After you've reached this level of awareness, it's time to follow the yellow brick road. You've made up your mind, you have a plan, and now it's time to execute. We're not saying that you won't have moments where you have to adjust the plan, but the process stays the same. Every pilot who flies an airplane needs to constantly make course corrections, but they get to their destination.

Every week, you need to take the broader goal and break it down into attainable wins that get you closer to your main objective. Once you learn to operate in this mode, the rest of your success will fall into place.

You may be reading this and thinking, "I want to learn how to make money in multifamily real estate." We will get to that soon, but without the right type of mindset, the remainder of your journey will be more challenging.

Remember, failure is only success deferred. Once we put our will to something, it's just a matter of time before we conquer that goal. It's a matter of just not giving up.

HOW TO SET GOALS

In goal setting, the power of pen-to-paper should never be underestimated. Writing down your goals and speaking them aloud will help your subconscious attain your objectives. But this does not mean that they are set in stone. Your goals should be constantly reviewed and updated to accommodate your vision, support your successes, and help you overcome your challenges.

Here are a few questions to ask yourself when setting a new goal:

1. What are ten things I want to accomplish this year?

2. What are my three most important goals?

3. What have I always wanted to do but been afraid to attempt?

4. How much money would I like to be earning after one year, after two years, after three years?

5. What do I see as my purpose in life?

6. What do I enjoy doing?

When researching goals, we begin by listing what we want to accomplish that year. Once we plan our yearly goals, we work backwards and break them down into six-month goals. Then we break them down to monthly goals. Finally, they're broken down into weekly goals.

To set up this system, we use the AIM SMART strategy.

You have to AIM toward achieving real estate goals that you set for yourself.

A - stands for acceptable. What is the minimum amount of work that you can do to achieve the goal?

I - is the **ideal**. What is the maximum amount that you can do?

M - is right in the **middle**. What is the realistic amount that you can do?

This will help you narrow down exactly what the range your goal is in. While it's important to aim for the ideal, you need to make sure that you stay within an acceptable range without giving up.

Once the goal is targeted, proceed with the SMART process. This will help you create a plan for attaining your goals.

S stands for specific.
What is the first step toward reaching that goal?

M is measurable.
How will you know when you've achieved the measure of success?

A is achievable.
Is this first step achievable? If it isn't, go back and revise step number one.

R is reasonable.
How reasonable is it to achieve the first step at this time?

T is time.
What is your time frame for completing the first step?

Once you've gone through the SMART process for that first step towards your goal, you can continue to use the process for each step along the way.

For example, at some point, you will need to start calling brokers. You can use AIM SMART to decide how you're going to achieve that goal efficiently. You might decide that it would be **acceptable** to call one, **ideal** to call five, and three would be right about in the **middle**.

Once you've decided what your goal is, use the **SMART** system to decide the steps you're going to take. You will **specifically** call five brokers. Is this goal **measurable?** Yes, you have a numeric goal. Is it **achievable?** Yes, you can call five brokers. Is it **reasonable** to do this now? Yes, you're ready to look for a broker to help you find a property. Do you have a **timeline?** Yes, by the end of the week.

An important part of this process is to have someone holding you accountable for each step. We'll keep each other accountable to our goals or involve ourselves in coaching programs so we have group support. Accountability allows us to achieve our goals efficiently. Whether it's a business partner, a loved one, or a trusted friend, find somebody who will not only support you but will hold you accountable.

It's also very important to keep your goals somewhere visible. Jake likes to keep three goals on the dashboard of his car so it's in his face each morning. You might try the same strategy, or put it on your mirror for when you get ready in the morning, or even on your cell phone. Figure out what works best for you to keep yourself focused on the target.

We all have 168 hours in every week. How we plan them and what we get done is all up to us. Jake sets up his week on Sunday night and plans his week out hour by hour. It may seem cumbersome at first, but once you start planning to do this, you'll know exactly what you need to do to execute your goals.

When you begin searching for a property, there are three things you have to do: you have to begin networking with brokers, you have to start looking at properties yourself, and you absolutely must start researching your market. Those are all goals that you could start planning in the very beginning of your foray into real estate investment.

As you can see, you can use the AIM SMART strategy to outline goals, small or large. This will help you to keep yourself on track and be efficient in reaching your goals.

FIND YOUR PURPOSE

One of our favorite authors, Zig Ziglar, once said, "Shoot for the stars. If you don't make it, at least you'll hit the moon". Unfortunately, most of us reach for the clouds, and are lucky to hit the ceiling.

If you understand your motivation, you'll put in that extra effort to reach for the stars. For some people money itself is a great motivator. For us, real estate gives us a sense of fulfillment.

A lot of our tenants don't have the option of buying their own homes; they have to rent an apartment. Providing clean, safe, affordable housing for tenants is one of our priorities. We make communities out of apartment buildings and we're pouring our blood, sweat, and tears into our work. Our tagline is "Modern Affordability." We want to bring value to the tenants. That's why we're able to charge higher rents; we offer quality service.

For example, our first property was drug-infested and crime-ridden. We cleaned it up, made it look nice, and called the cops on some tenants. Several months later, we sent out surveys and the response was incredible. People told us that it finally felt like home.

This work allows us to make a difference. As you get older in life, it's important to find something that fulfills you. If you're doing something that you really enjoy, you have so much energy. You'll challenge yourself creatively. You'll want to work and you will become so much more productive.

Don't get us wrong, work is always going to feel like work. But, overall, it's important to enjoy what you're doing; if you don't, what's the point? Working in real estate is fun for us. It's challenging, but gives us the freedom to set our own schedule. We hope to give you the tools and knowledge you need to break down the barrier of fear, and achieve your goals.

WHEELBARROW INVESTING

Napoleon Hill once said, "knowledge is not power; knowledge is only potential power. It becomes power only when and if it is organized into definite plans of action and directed to a definite end." This is where our proven wheelbarrow investing system comes into play.

In order to use a wheelbarrow, you must have 2 legs and a functioning wheel. If any of these parts fail, your wheelbarrow collapses. Multifamily investing is also dependent on 3 functioning parts: buy right, manage right, and finance right. If any of these parts fail, like the wheelbarrow, your multifamily investment has a potential to collapse.

The remainder of this book will focus on our proven system. We will show you how to buy right, manage right, and finance right. With all these parts in place, you ensure the success of your investment. The goal is to fill your wheelbarrow with apartment buildings that provide long-term profits.

CHAPTER 3 SUMMARY

Jake and Gino's 3P's for Real Estate Success

1. Plan – if you don't know where you are going, how will you get there?

2. Persistence - We've been rejected hundreds of times. Don't quit!

3. Patience – The beginning of your multifamily career is going to seem like a pipe dream but if you work every day, you will get there. Once your snowball picks up steam you will be amazed at how quickly your wealth skyrockets.

Time for action

1. What's your plan?

2. What are you doing today to get closer to goal?

3. Do your goals make you nervous? Quick tip - If your goals don't make you nervous, they aren't big enough.

Check out www.jakeandgino.com for more wealth building tips

CHAPTER 4

HOW TO CHOOSE YOUR MARKET

Beginning a new venture can be daunting, but with the right knowledge it can also be incredibly rewarding. We speak with a lot of new investors, and usually the first question they ask is "Where do I start?" The best way to achieve success is to have knowledge on your side, and that's what this chapter is all about. We'll teach you where to invest, how to choose a market, and most importantly, how to select an ideal property. So let's get started!

WHERE TO INVEST?

Real estate policies and taxes vary in the United States from one state and region to the next, so it's important to do your homework on the laws where you're beginning your venture.

We had several practical reasons for investing in Tennessee, the most obvious being that Jake had recently relocated to Knoxville, but there are also many advantages to investing in real estate in that city and state.

First, it's a beautiful area, so that helps when trying to rent a property. Secondly, eviction policies are typically more favorable to landlords in our area, which works in our favor when we have to deal with a problem tenant. The eviction proceedings move along relatively quickly in our market, averaging 30 days. In certain other states, you might be waiting 90 - 120 days to evict someone, and during that time you won't be collecting any rent from the current tenant and have no chance of renting to another person.

We were also attracted to the demographics of the market. At the time, there was a good job growth rate along with a strong population of blue-collar workers. We knew that this demographic would constitute our customer base, and most complexes in the area at the time weren't catering to blue-collar families. We purchased a complex across the street from a manufacturing plant that employs 4,500 workers. We met with their HR and created a lasting relationship. Our motto is "modern affordability." We strive to offer safe, clean, and affordable units to hard working people.

This was confirmed when we received the results of our tenant surveys and the most consistent compliment we received was that we cared about the property and the needs of the tenants. All of these qualifications made Knoxville the ideal market in which to begin investing.

RESEARCHING EMERGING MARKETS

Knoxville as an emerging market. We are currently looking to expand our portfolio to other emerging markets, such as Florida. We believe that you should either invest close to home for obvious reasons such as hands on ability to resolve problems, visibility, and convenience or select an emerging market to take advantage of rising values (buy cheap and sell high), job expansion, and population growth.

When you're ready to start your search for a property, the first step is to type the name of a city into a search engine. From population growth to employment figures, you can learn almost anything about a city with just a few clicks. Next, weigh the positives and negatives about the market and evaluate if it's worth a trip to investigate further. When we find a market that's appealing, we'll schedule a trip. Our goal is to visit with as many property managers, brokers, lenders, and potential sellers as possible so we have a good understanding of people living in the market.

While you can find most of your required information through a simple Internet search, if you're looking for more in-depth data two of the best places to go are the U.S. Bureau of Labor and Statistics and the city's official website. Below are four specific things to look for when choosing where to invest.

1. **Job growth**: This is the first indication of an emerging market. It's important to remember that jobs are a large driving force when it comes to where people are deciding to live. It also tends to have a multiplier effect, meaning when one white-collar job is created, between two and five additional blue-collar jobs typically follow. We like to see at least 2% job growth for two consecutive years. When demand increases, so does rent. Remember that it will take a few months for rent to catch up with an emerging job market, but you're investing in steady, future profits. That's why we like to have the property located where there's a concentration of jobs, such as a university, shopping mall, or a manufacturing plant.

2. **Construction:** This is a good indicator of a market's trajectory. Building permits are often issued a year before construction begins and are easily found through public record. These records can be easily accessed by going to the town hall. If you research the permits, you can see the path of progress for many cities. This is where new construction and growth is ongoing. You can also look to major retailers and new infrastructure. Also, look for cities or neighborhoods in which revitalization efforts are taking place. Once you see a jump in construction for two or

three years, you'll witness the market building up. Your broker might also know this type of information, so be sure to ask them.

3. **Households**: It's important to see if the number of households is rising in a specific area because when demand in a certain sub-market increases, rents rise. Keep in mind that there's a difference between the *number of households* and *population*. The latter will tell you the number of people in a city, while the former will let you know how many potential groups of renters there are. When the number of households decreases, the demand for rentals will also drop and rates will follow.

4. **Demographics**: It's important to identify a specific demographic for your tenant base. Look for a higher population of people in their 20's-30's or those who are 55 and up. Those who are middle age tend to have families and are more prone to purchas-ing a home rather than renting an apartment. You're also going to want to look for areas where the population is largely single and where the families are younger and smaller. Your goal is to have a group of people who are going to rent.

We often encourage novice investors to purchase their first property within a thirty-minute drive of their home whenever possible. It's better and easier to jump in the car and drive to the property if a problem arises than to jump on a plane to assess the situation.

THE POWER OF THE SUB-MARKET

Once you've assessed the market, turn your attention to filtering down your search. When we decided to invest in Knoxville, we concentrated on the sub-market in the South End. By focusing on a sub-market, you'll be able to eliminate countless properties and make your search much more manageable. Typically, we look for sub-markets that have a population of 30,000 or more, that are growing, and that are located near a large city. Because our target niche tenant base is comprised of blue-collar workers, we like to identify areas that are known for manufacturing with booming new retail stores.

In our experience, we've sometimes been able to purchase apartment units in these areas for *half of the price* of comparable units located in the heart of the neighboring metro area. These sub-markets are usually able to command rents within $50-$100 of the nearby metro area, making it an extremely promising investment. Additionally, if you can identify a sub-market outside of the city limits, you'll be able to avoid city taxes.

MEETING WITH YOUR BROKER

It's always beneficial to have concluded your analysis of the market prior to your visit. That way, when you meet with your broker, you'll be able to ask the right questions. Don't hesitate to write up a list of questions, which should include:

- What are the market rents for a typical unit?
- What is the per-unit cost of an apartment in the market?
- What is the occupancy rate in the market currently?
- If you're speaking with a broker about a specific listing, you should ask:
- Could you describe the tenant base? Are they employed? Do they receive government assistance? How do they obtain their income?
- Do tenants pay on time?
- Is it run by a professional management company?
- What are the big businesses in this area?

The only way to locate a superior property is to become an expert in that market, and doing extensive research can help get you there.

TYPICAL STEPS IN ACQUIRING A PROPERTY

Once you've determined what sub-market you'd like to invest in, it's time to start researching which property you'd like to purchase. Below are the typical steps in acquiring a property:

1. Choose market/begin research

2. Contact brokers

3. Start to build a team

4. Begin analyzing deals

5. Figure out strategy:

    a. Long term hold

    b. Buy and flip

    c. Buy, reposition, and sell

    d. Buy, reposition, and refinance

6. 100-10-1. Analyze 100 properties – Bid on 10 – Acquire 1.

7. Write Letter of Intent

8. Negotiate and begin to acquire financing

9. Create purchase and sale agreement (Contract)

10. Perform due diligence

11. Renegotiate

12. Close

13. Start operation of property

We use several websites to begin our research in a chosen market:

- Loopnet
- Local commercial real estate websites
- The websites for the local real estate associations

Loopnet is an excellent resource for locating brokers, as you'll be able to compare the brokers listing these properties. Most listings in a market are dominated by a few top-producing brokers, and these are the professionals you want to call. It may take a few conversations to establish a relationship with a broker, so we use a script to explain our investment criteria. We also send them our credibility tool kit, which outlines our business plan and experience.

Brokers are key members of your team. They can bring you deals before they hit the market, thus allowing for less competition and a lower purchase price. They've established relationships with banks, mortgage brokers, sellers, and other real estate brokers who can deliver to them these deals. Meeting a good broker early on can provide endless marketing opportunities.

This is the script we use when introducing ourselves to a broker:

Hi, my name is (your name). I'm an investor in the (city, state) area and I'm looking to purchase apartment buildings in your market. My preference is buying B to C type properties that contain between 30 and 150 units with at least a 10% cash-on-cash return and a cap rate of at least 8%. I specialize in purchasing apartments that are run by mom-and-pops. Would you happen to have any properties that fit these criteria?

When looking for brokers, it's better to cast a wide net. Be sure to send an introductory letter off to as many qualified brokers as possible. However, don't think that finding a good broker is the only way to find a property. There are other avenues to locate deals, including:

1. **Classified ads:** To be successful with classifieds, diligence is key. Scour the ads every day to see if anything pops up. In our market, we have a publication called the Pennysaver that advertises all types of properties for sale. It's challenging to come across a good deal, but perusing the classifieds will give you an idea of what's available in the market. Most "For Sale By Owners" (FSBO) properties are advertised in this type of media, along with real estate agents who are trying to elicit phone calls from potential customers. You can even place your own ad in the paper that details what you're looking for. This is a great strategy because if someone does call on your ad, you'll know that you are dealing with a serious prospect. If you do this, be sure to make the ad compelling and include your website if you have one so the potential seller can check your credibility.

2. **For Sale by Owner:** A person who lists their property without the advice and guidance of a broker is taking a huge risk. Brokers give the property more exposure, along with an accurate assessment of the current market value. Brokers can pre-qualify buyers to make sure that they qualify for bank financing. You may be able to locate a property that's undervalued when sold directly by the owner. Keep in mind that it's important to use a broker whenever selling your property to ensure you get the highest price.

3. **Direct Mailings:** Direct mail can be an effective tool for locating properties that are not currently for sale. There are two strategies that most real estate investors use to find the addresses of property owners. You can either call the assessor's office in your city or acquire the information, or they hire a list broker to provide the addresses. Macromark is a list broker that we've used in the

past, and they've provided us with excellent lists tailored to our specific needs. They are located in New York.

If you want to be successful with direct mailings, you'll have to be persistent and consistent. Mailings should be sent out at least every three months and sent to the same owners. An owner may not be ready to sell their property in June, but circumstances may change and your letter in October could spur them into action. The problem with direct mailings is that they may generate a rather low response rate, usually between 1% and 2%.

If you send out 100 letters, then you can hope to receive one or two serious prospects. Have a team member or intern help you with sending out the mail pieces. Use colored envelopes to catch the attention of the prospect. On the next page, you'll find our direct mailer template.

(Your name)

(Your address)

(Name of property owner)

(Address)

Dear (Sir/ Madam):

My partner and I are interested in buying income property in your area. We currently own several properties and feel that yours would be an excellent addition to our portfolio. You can find out more about who we are at (insert website).

We're not looking to list your property as brokers, rather to buy your property outright, thus saving you commission costs and allowing you to get top dollar.

We would be interested in assuming a loan or owner financing. However, we can make a substantial down payment if the price and terms are attractive. We completely understand if you're not willing to sell your property yet, and we'll follow up with you at a later date if we do not hear back from you. Should you find our offer promising, please don't hesitate to give us a call at (phone number).

Thank you for your time, and we look forward to hearing from you.

Sincerely,

P.S. There is NO commission and NO expensive appraisal, just a fair price.

Team Members to Help You With Your Search

Having a broker on your team will ensure that there's someone who knows exactly what you're looking for, and they'll be able to look for a property that matches your criteria. Brokers can be especially valuable to you as time goes on, however, they're by no means the only team members with the ability to locate deals.

Here's a list of professionals that can help you with your search:

- Accountants
- Property Managers
- Insurance Agents
- Financial Planners
- Mortgage Brokers
- Bankers
- Lawyers
- Inspectors

While you're rounding out your team, you can ask the team members that you already have to help you with your search. For example, if you found a broker that you like working with, you can ask them if they know any good lawyers or accountants. Having a solid team will not only give you peace of mind, it will help lead you to success.

Persistence and Credibility

Tenacity is hard to maintain, but it's worth it. We believe in the 100-10-1 principal, especially for beginners. **100** is the amount of properties you'll have to analyze to find **10** that might be worth while, and you'll only close on **1** of those deals. This number will drop drastically as you gain experience in the market. We got so beat up in the beginning because there was so much rejection. For a year and a half, our efforts gave us *nothing.* But once we bought our first property and received credibility, our success began to snowball. In the last 18 months, we've acquired over $10 million in multifamily real estate. The most intelligent thing we've done is keep going despite adversity. We never quit. Patience and persistence, along with good research, is going to be one of the keys to achieving success in multifamily real estate investing.

CHAPTER 4 SUMMARY

Traits that we look for when selecting a market

1.) Areas with a high concentration of our niche tenants

    a. (Blue-collar manufacturing and retail workers)

2.) Submarkets

3.) High growth area

Time for Action

1.) What type of market are you looking for?

2.) Who is already on your team, and who else have you identified as a potential teammate?"

3.) What markets have you currently identified?

Check out www.jakeandgino.com for more wealth building tips

CHAPTER 5

BUILDING YOUR TEAM

Now that you've identified your market and begun identifying potential properties, it's time to start building your team. Most business deals are the result of good relationships, and buying multifamily housing is no different. As you develop your team of professionals, people may start bringing you unexpected deals or giving you tips on how to run your business more efficiently. When your team is in place, closing on a property becomes easier. You'll be able to pick up the phone and call your inspector, banker, or insurance agent and give them the run down of your new investment. By that time, you'll have a good understanding of their fees, so negotiation will be minimal. As your multifamily portfolio grows, so will your team, and the investing process becomes much easier.

PRIMARY TEAM MEMBERS

Before you begin putting together your team, it's important to know which professionals are necessary for acquiring a property. We've drafted a checklist that will help with your search:

1. Lawyer/Title Company

2. Broker

3. Accountant

4. Mortgage Broker

5. Insurance Broker

6. Property Inspector

7. Handymen

8. Management Company

9. Tenant Background Check System

10. Construction Contractors

11. Laundry Company

12. RUBS company

13. Website Specialist / Photographer

14. Renters Insurance Company

15. Cost Segregation Consultant

16. Coach

Each of the aforementioned professionals provides you with valuable services and information. However, finding the right ones can be a challenge. In our experience, creating a team requires a lot of due diligence to ensure that you're finding the best people for the project and for you.

LAWYER

Depending on where you purchase real estate, a lawyer may have to be used to execute the purchase and sale agreement. Even if they're not, it's important to use a lawyer for creating and reviewing all necessary legal documents, including operating agreements, purchase and sale agreements, and property management agreements. A lawyer will also be able to provide other template documents, such as leases, and can help file the correct forms for your Limited Liability Company (LLC).

REAL ESTATE BROKER

It would be wise to build relationships with a few brokers instead of just one. Don't hesitate to spend some time with them when you're first getting to know them. Take them out to lunch and ask them questions about the market and any potential deals on the horizon. While you're getting to know them, be on the lookout for any red flags that something just isn't right. For example, if the broker starts talking about a particular listing, ask questions about the property to determine whether or not it actually exists or if it is a viable deal. Run the other way if the broker insists or asks you to sign an exclusivity agreement.

It's important that your broker also send you the tax return numbers, not just the proforma figures. View proforma figures as projected or wishful thinking. Only buy on actuals. Don't let them try to take advantage of you just because you're a new investor. They may not even let you visit the property in an attempt to get you to make an offer prior to your property tour, but that's an extremely ill-advised move.

Keep in mind that it's the broker's responsibility to know the market. If they're not getting the market rent numbers for you or any other finan-cial numbers you ask for, they're not doing their job.

1. How long have you been a real estate agent?
Here are some questions to ask a potential broker:

2. What type of real estate do you specialize in?

3. Do you sell multifamily properties, single-family, commercial, etc.?

4. Do you invest in properties yourself?

5. Do you work with investors?

6. How many listings do you currently have on the market?

7. How much real estate did you sell last year?

8. Can you identify the path of progress in your market?

9. What is the cap rate in your market?

10. Can you recommend any professionals for my team, such as accountants, lawyers, or other insurance agents?

Once you get an honest and reliable broker, finding qualified properties becomes much easier. We were fortunate enough to work with Rick Gentry as the listing broker for our first real estate acquisition. When we closed on the property, Rick didn't disappear like most brokers do when the commission check is deposited. Instead, he helped transition the property over to us and was there to answer any questions we had. Naturally, when it came time to put an offer on our next property we called him first.

It's imperative that you locate a broker who specializes in multifamily investing. Rick was able to give us insight into the local market and analyze the financials of the property because he understood exactly what we needed. His responsibilities also entailed running rent comps and helping us build our team. He even reached out to companies and acquired repair quotes for certain jobs on our second property. To this day, when we have a question or something comes up that we're not familiar with, we give Rick a call.

Since our first deal with Rick, he's brought us a few very profitable listings. Because we're reliable closers, brokers will occasionally bring off market deals (also referred to as pocket listings) directly to us. It will definitely take time to build your credibility, but eventually the good deals will start finding you instead of the other way around.

ACCOUNTANT

A quality accountant is a vital member of your team. They help you maintain your records, look for cost-saving strategies, and help you save money on your taxes. The following are eight questions to ask any accountant you're looking to hire:

1. Can you give me an example of a tax saving strategy that you use?

2. Do you have any other clients that invest in real estate?

3. Do you own any investment properties yourself?

4. What is your opinion on owning real estate?

5. In what type of entity do you like to hold real estate?

6. Do you work with any Section 1031 intermediaries?

7. Can you recommend a bookkeeper?

8. Do you perform cost segregation studies or can you refer us to someone who does?

It is vital that your accountant either own real estate investments or have clients who own real estate.

Mortgage Broker

Through our mortgage broker, we've had great success working with local banks to get financing. There are several advantages to working with local banks over big banks. Because all of their decisions are made locally, you won't be stuck waiting for a decision to come in from out of state. They're also in tune with your local market and market values. They generally have more flexibility than larger institutions, and if you establish a relationship, they could present you with deals.

Because we typically buy distressed properties, we prefer to use community banks for recourse loans out front because they are very knowledgeable about the local market and are much easier to work with. After we've rehabbed and repositioned the property, we utilize the mortgage broker to get us a non-recourse, long-term fixed loan when we refinance.

Insurance Broker

An insurance broker will provide you with the proper coverage on your property. They should be knowledgeable about the market and offer advice on what types of coverage you'll need. Additionally, they can offer business insurance to offset the loss of rental income in case you lose part of the building.

As with your other team members, make sure that you're choosing someone who deals with multifamily housing. Insuring single-family homes is a totally different insurance market; if you lose your house that you live in, your income is still secure. However, when you lose your investment, you have to insure against the loss of income. Whenever we buy a new property, we have two insurance brokers compete against one another to receive the best pricing.

Side note: it's vital to have a yearly review of all policies to ensure that you have the proper coverage for your property and to keep the cost of the insurance competitive.

PROPERTY INSPECTOR

You have to make sure that your inspector is thorough. It shouldn't matter if you have one hundred units or one thousand, make sure they get into every unit. This ensures that if you find anything wrong, you'll be able to notify the previous owner and get it fixed on their dime. Whatever they find will be worth the fee and then some.

Getting the property inspected is the first thing you should do when you get the contract and the financing secured. Without the inspection, there's not much else you can do. It's standard for the inspector to charge per unit, and you'll want to book them at least two weeks in advance since their appointment slots tend to fill up quickly.

www.homeinspector.org is a resource for finding property inspectors.

HANDYMEN

These guys are the front line of your operation. Out of all of your team members, handymen directly impact the customer service end of your business. Courteous and competent handymen keep your tenants happy, and happy tenants will stick around longer. If your handyman is slow or rude, you can be sure that your existing tenants will start looking for another apartment. Running an apartment complex is just like any other business. Customer service is a key component to your success.

MANAGEMENT COMPANY

Managing a property is often overlooked by first time investors. Once the property is purchased, it's tempting to think that the job is done. The truth is, once you've acquired a property, that's when the real work begins.

If you decide to run your own properties, you should still interview management companies to familiarize yourself with costs associated with running each investment. Remember, if you're not managing your property correctly, there's a good chance it's going to fail just like any other business. This is why you need to hire a good management company to take care of your properties if you decide not to self-manage the property.

For more information on selecting a management company go to jakeandgino.com and pick up a copy of our eBook "To Manage or Not to Manage."

Tenant Background Check System

The biggest mistake new property owners make is neglecting to do background checks on prospective tenants. Do yourself a favor and do them every time. You might be tempted to say, "I have a gut feeling about this tenant." Even if you're good at reading people, you'll still be wrong once in a while, and it's a nightmare to get a tenant out once they're already in and settled.

Background checks should not be optional, not just for your own safety, but for that of your tenants. For example, you don't want to have a sexual predator living on the property. It's even important to do a background check if you know the tenants personally. You might be surprised to see what's on their record. We perform criminal and credit checks on each tenant and charge an application fee to cover the cost.

Contractors and Rehab Services

To protect yourself from liability, it's critical to employ a contractor who's licensed and insured. We like to ask our team members for referrals when hiring contractors, and prefer to hire small local companies who will share our vision for enhancing the community. They will also be able to offer more competitive pricing due to lower overhead.

You'll require several contractors while rehabbing your apartments. Below is a short list of who you might need:

1. Lawn care

2. Painters

3. Plumber

4. Fence Company

5. Paving Company

6. Roofer

7. General Carpentry and Maintenance

8. Carpet Cleaner

9. Flooring Company

10. Used Appliance Company

11. Window Company

12. Electrician

To ensure you're getting the best price for the quality, make sure to get three to five different bids for each job. We had four painting jobs that needed to be done within this past year, and we ran through multiple companies before we found one that was reliable for a fair price. When the job was complete, we set up a fixed pricing system with them. Now we know exactly what it's going to cost us to paint our units, which is very useful when it comes to budgeting.

The only caveat to using a contractor is that once the job is finished, you *must* pay them in full. If the contractor gets a call from you as well as another building owner, who are they going to service first? They're going to go with who pays them on time, every time.

When you use the same contractor consistently, it's relatively easy to set up fixed pricing. It takes a quick conversation and it's a major perk. For example, our plumber gives us a steep discount. Should anything happen, like a water heater breaks, its $99. Usually, it would cost a lot more, but because we provide them with a lot of business, we can lock in fixed pricing.

LAUNDRY COMPANY

We utilize a company that provides new laundry machines to our properties. They take care of all the maintenance and collections on the machines, then split the income with our company.

When we bought our second property, we took the machines out and we sold them. We made money on the sale of the old machines and we had the laundry company come in and install brand new ones at no additional cost.

It's a great set up. If there's a problem with any machine, our property manager uses an app on his phone to scan the code on the machine. In turn, this alerts the company so they can send a tech out to repair it. It's an especially helpful process because it allows our maintenance staff to focus on other aspects of the property.

Check out www.coinmach.com or www.caldwellandgregory.com

RUBS

RUBS, which stands for Ratio Utility Billing System, is a water bill-back service that we use to cut down on the cost of running the property. The RUBS system works by using the existing water meter to measure consumption, and then specialized software breaks it down to estimate the usage per unit. Two bedroom units would be charged a higher amount than one bedroom units. Most of our buildings were built decades ago when they installed a master meter for the entire building. Rather than install sub-meters for every apartment, RUBS allows you to bill for utilities per-unit so you don't have to install brand new meters.

It's important to note that you shouldn't install RUBS if it's not the industry standard in your market. If your competition isn't using it, then you might get some push-back from your tenants.

You might even consider capping the amount a tenant would have to pay. For example, we cap ours at $35 because that's what the market typically does in East Tennessee, but this varies depending on the region. When setting up RUBS, make sure to ask your team members detailed questions about how it's commonly used in your area.

If you successfully implement RUBS and receive an extra $30 a month with 30 units, you'll have an extra $900 a month. That means you'll generate around $10,800 a year in additional income.

There are huge environmental benefits as well, considering that RUBS tends to reduce the tenant's water usage. If a tenant knows they're paying every time they use water, they're more conscientious of how much they use. It's going to save you money and have a positive environmental impact.

Google search RUBS companies for more information.

WEBSITE SPECIALIST / PHOTOGRAPHER

Hiring a website specialist and a photographer is an inexpensive way to add credibility to your company. One of the only marketing fees we pay for is the hosting of our websites. We were lucky enough to find a web developer who doubles as our photographer, so he includes free photo shoots of our properties for our websites. Most of the mom-and-pop operations that we take over don't have a web presence, which greatly reduces the amount of prospective tenants who might discover them.

The best thing you can do to your website is have professional photos taken as they tend to make it look so much more professional. Below is a checklist of what you should have on your website:

- Professional photos of the property

- Professional photos of a model unit

- Floor plans

- The amenities you offer

- Contact information

As your company grows, you might want to consider adding a mainte-nance request form or even setting up an online payment system.

RENTERS INSURANCE

This is an easy way to get some additional funds. The more renters we get to sign up, the bigger the bonus we get from the renters insurance company for marketing their services. Also, if the tenant trashes the unit, the renters insurance will cover your repair costs. It's a win-win for everyone involved. Your tenants can purchase renters insurance through your existing broker.

SIGN COMPANY

We usually rename apartment complexes after we take over so the ownership change is visible. The sign company typically won't design the logo for you, but there are several websites that can cover that, such as elance, 99 designs or crowdspring. After we have our new logo, we order new signs to begin changing the image of the property.

COST SEGREGATION CONSULTANT

Cost segregation generally works with much larger properties. This process begins by segregating the assets of the property, such as the refrigerators, air conditioning units, or hot water heaters, all of which have a different cost basis. These all depreciate much faster than the property, which means you can write off more on your taxes.

Once this is complete, the primary goal of a cost segregation study is to identify all construction-related costs that depreciate over a shorter tax life, typically around five, seven, or nine years instead of the standard 27.5 years for a multifamily. It helps save on personal income taxes, which is why it's important to have an accountant on your team who understands cost segregation. If your accountant has experience in cost segregation studies, you're all set. However, they may recommend bringing in a consultant if they don't offer such services themselves.

The analysis itself is not cheap. We spent about $10,000 for our last study, but it all comes back to you in the long run. These assets depreciate at a much faster rate, and the write off will be huge, so it's worth it. When you go through this process, you must follow the IRS guidelines. This ensures that, should you ever be audited, you'll have the report and it'll show line by line what you're segregating and how you came up with those figures.

When you're selecting a cost segregation study, you'll want to utilize the engineering method because it's the most compreh therefore, the preferred methodology of the IRS. It's the safest and provides us with the maximum tax write off. A good cost segregation team member can provide tremendous value.

COACH

There are different types of coaches you could use. For example, we've utilized real estate coaches, business coaches, and financial coaches. They help you develop a plan, provide guidance, and most importantly, will hold you accountable for your actions. Gino found coaching to be so vital to his personal growth that he decided to attend the Institute of Professional Excellence in Coaching (IPEC), and became a certified professional coach.

Go to www.jakeandgino.com for more information on coaching.

TEAMWORK

Collaboration and teamwork are essential. When we work as a team, we leverage each individual's skills and we're capable of getting more done. Although team building might seem counter-intuitive to someone who wants to do everything themselves, when you become an entrepreneur, you'll find out just how vital it is.

The quality of your team determines whether or not you'll be successful. Part of being a team leader is to empower your team members to use their strengths. If you have a competent team around you that feel like they can give their input and be both heard and respected, you'll be able to get things accomplished that you wouldn't be able to do on your own.

Once you have a solid and reliable team, every property purchase will be just like pushing a button. Everyone will know their role and everything will be more efficient. You'll know who to call and that you can rely on them. In every sense, looking at your investment as a team effort is the best way to run your business.

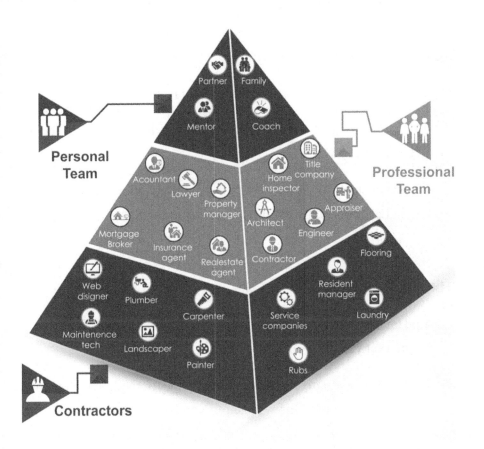

CHAPTER 5 SUMMARY

Building Your Team

1.) Get to know every multifamily broker in your market.

2.) When you find a good broker, they will help you build the rest of your team.

3.) Never stop recruiting. We always ask who other people are using and are constantly evaluating our team members.

Time for Action

1.) Have you cultivated a relationship with the brokers in your market yet?

2.) Have you created an investment book to share with potential team members? This will help if you lack credibility.

3.) Have you made all of the people in your inner circle aware of your plans? Your inner circle may have some good referrals for you.

Check out www.jakeandgino.com for more wealth building tips

CHAPTER 6

HOW TO SPEAK THE LANGUAGE

While learning the terms in this chapter is a necessary evil, it's absolutely necessary to master them. Brokers won't take you seriously until you can speak the language. Utilize this chapter as reference guide.

The real estate industry has a language all its own, and it's one you're going to have to both learn and apply if you want to be successful in this business.

It may seem intimidating at first, but it's just like if you were to learn any another language. The more you practice, the better you're going to be at it. Before long, it will become second nature to you.

Our deal analyzer software, which is available on our member site at wheelbarrowprofits.com, will take care of most of your calculations, but you'll still need to understand what the terminology used actually means. Keep reading to become familiar with some of the basic language of multifamily real estate investing.

GROSS SCHEDULED INCOME (GSI)/GROSS POTENTIAL INCOME (GPI)

This can be defined as the cumulative rent for all of the units in a property, including those that are not currently generating revenue.

VACANCY ALLOWANCE

The percentage of vacancy expected is the Vacancy Allowance. It's the amount of missing rent due to unrented apartments and uncollectable rent that's anticipated by the bank. The Vacancy Allowance is useful in adjusting the appraisal analysis for typical vacancy in a given market. The rule of thumb for banks is about a 5% vacancy allowance, but it may be higher depending on your market conditions.

GROSS OPERATING INCOME (GOI)

The GOI is the annual rental income collected from all occupied units, as well as income from other sources, such as laundry and storage. To calculate this amount, subtract the Vacancy Allowance from the GSI and add any other income sources.

> *Gross Scheduled Income*
> *- Vacancy and Credit Loss*
> *+ Other income*
> _____
> *= Gross Operating Income*

NET OPERATING INCOME (NOI)

The most important figure in valuing an income producing property is the NOI, which is calculated by subtracting the operating expense from the GOI. The NOI is essential because it's the amount left over prior to your mortgage expense, making it the real value of the property. Your objective in real estate is to grow your NOI as high as possible. You have to remember that you're buying an income stream, not just a property. It doesn't matter if you have granite countertops or a magnificent view, as long as your property has a rising NOI you're accomplishing your goal.

Gross Operating Income

- Operating Expenses

= Net Operating Income

OPERATING EXPENSES

This can be characterized as any expense related to running the property, such as utilities, repairs, landscaping, or garbage removal.

CAPITALIZATION RATE (CAP RATE)

The cap rate is the rate of return you expect to receive on a property, excluding any debt service. What is debt service? Debt service is the cash required to cover the repayment of principal and interest for a particular time period. The cap rate is used to determine the asset's current value without any leverage on the asset. In order to determine the cap rate of a property, you're going to need to first know the NOI. Additionally, cap rates have an inverse relationship. A higher cap rate denotes a lower price and vice versa. As always, your goal should be to drive down the selling price when closing a deal. This will drive your Cap Rate higher without needing to increase your NOI.

The cap rate is calculated as follows:

If a building has an NOI of $50,000 and it's selling for $500,000, then the cap rate would be 50,000/500,000 = 10%.

You can also determine the value of an asset by dividing the NOI by the cap rate:

A building with an NOI of $100,000 and a cap rate of 10% would have a value of $1 million.

It's vital that you determine the average cap rates for multifamily properties in your market. Call a few brokers to gauge the cap rate for the market. This is just one of the barometers we use to analyze a deal, and we always strive to buy properties with a cap rate of at least 8%.

$$\text{Cap Rate} = \frac{NOI}{Value\ (Sales\ Price)}$$

CAPITAL EXPENDITURES (CAPEX)

A CapEx is different from everyday expenses or repairs. It's an improvement, such as adding a new roof or paving a driveway, that extends the useful life of an existing asset for a period of more than one year.

It's important to note how a CapEx differs from a repair. The latter restores an asset to its original condition after damage, but it doesn't significantly extend the usefulness of the asset. For example, when you replace a roof, that's a CapEx, but when you're replacing shingles on the roof, that's a repair.

When you run a property, you must establish a CapEx fund. A rule of thumb for this fund would be to put aside $250 per unit per year (or $21 per unit per month) so that when a refrigerator has to be replaced or a parking lot needs to be paved you'll have the cash available. For example, a property with 30 units should allocate $625 per month (or $7,500 per year) for the CapEx fund.

Not creating a CapEx fund was one of our earlier mistakes, one that you can learn from so you don't have to deal with it yourself. We woke up one day to discover that our septic fields at Courtyard Cottages had to be replaced and the funds had to be siphoned from our monthly cash flow. It cost us a huge amount of money, and even though we were fortunate that we could pay for the repair with our existing funds, we could have easily been out of business in an instant. We used a plumber who allowed us to pay him off over several months.

Another advantage of setting up a CapEx fund is that it proves to the bank that you're responsible. When you're ready to refinance the property, it shows the banks that your company is credible and that you're well prepared to protect yourselves from unforeseeable disasters.

CASH-ON-CASH RETURN

We tend to look for properties that yield cash-on-cash returns of at least 10%. However, in order to syndicate your deal to investors, you'll need a minimum of 12%. A real estate syndication is when investors pool their money together to buy bigger properties. To calculate cash-on-cash return, take the annual cash income and divide it by the total cash invested.

Example: If you receive $10,000 in cash flow and you invested $100,000 in cash, then your return would be 10,000/100,000 = 10%. We strive to put in as little of our capital as possible in order to obtain the highest cash-on-cash return.

$$Cash\ on\ Cash = \frac{Cash\ Flow}{Total\ Cash\ Invested}$$

DEBT SERVICE COVERAGE RATIO (DSCR)

The DSCR is the ratio between the NOI and the annual debt service, and it's the calculation banks use when deciding about qualifying the property for a loan. It exposes whether or not the property will be able to cover the mortgage and bills. A DSCR of 1.0 indicates that you have just enough money to pay the mortgage, and anything lower than 1.0 means that you'll come up short on the mortgage payment. Banks normally like to see a figure of at least 1.2, however, we don't buy a property unless it's at least 1.3.

$$DSCR = \frac{NOI}{Annual\ Debt\ Service}$$

PROPERTY RATINGS

Brokers will rate properties from A to D with A being the highest and D being the lowest. The type of property that you're buying will definitely affect the cap rate.

"A" PROPERTIES: They'll typically be newer and inhabited by white-collar workers. Institutions usually buy "A" properties because they'll stay consistent, but there isn't much room for growth. Because they don't need to be repositioned, they aren't necessarily vehicles for creating wealth, but can aid in maintaining wealth. They'll have the greatest appreciation, but the worst cash flow. "A" properties are usually less risky, but yield fewer rewards as a result.

"B" PROPERTIES: Built within the last 20-30 years, the property will show its age with a bit of deferred maintenance or functional obsolescence. You may see older heating and cooling systems, roofs that have a bit of wear and tear, and parking lots in need of repair. Our 136-unit property in Knoxville fell into this category. It was around 20 years old, and even though the previous owners elected to defer maintenance, we were glad to take on the work and restore it to its former glory. These properties tend to have a mix of blue and white-collar workers, and are easy to reposition if they have some deferred maintenance. They tend to have a good mix of cash flow and appreciation.

"C" PROPERTIES: Usually at least 30 years old, they house mostly blue-collar workers and possibly Section 8 (subsidized housing) tenants. Once you find a good tenant, they usually stay for a long period of time

because they don't often end up buying their own home. It's usually a good idea to buy a "C" property when it has deferred maintenance. If you perform the deferred maintenance and manage the property well, then you will be creating what investors refer to as "forcing appreciation." That's the investment sweet spot. "C" properties have great cash flow, but appreciation is limited unless forced.

"D" PROPERTIES: These properties are typically in areas that have major problems, and the properties usually reflect that. For example, there may be drug dealers on the property, tenants that don't pay, or there's a lot of damage. Unless you're willing to buy a "D" property and reposition it to a "C" property, we recommend staying away from these listings. If the neighborhood has potential but the property is a mess, and you're willing to put the time, effort, and money into turning it around, then you may be able to raise it to a "C" property.

When it comes to cap rates, "A" properties have the lowest ranging from 3% to 5% while "B" properties are in the range of 6% to 8%. "C" properties hover in the 8%+ range, and "D" properties are 13%+. Just remember, a 15% cap rate looks great on paper, but it means nothing if you can't collect rent.

Cash Flow

Cash flow is the life-blood of any business.

Net Operating Income
- Debt Services
- Capital Expenditures
_____
Cash Flow (Before Taxes)

LOAN-TO-VALUE

The ratio between the mortgage of a property and the purchase price is the loan-to-value. Banks are typically willing to lend up to 80% of the property's value.

Example: A property with a loan amount of $800,000 and a value of $1 million would have a loan-to-value ratio of 80%. In this case, the most you would be able to borrow from the bank would be $800,000.

Leveraging is one of the best aspects of real estate. It allows buyers to get a $1 million property for $100,000 in the way that they only have to pay $200,000 for the down payment and can mortgage the rest of it. That's the beauty of leveraging; you can control a greater amount of income for a significantly smaller investment.

Teachable Moment: The down payment is always negotiable. We strive to find community banks that will allow us to put down 15%, and we've always been able to do so. In one of our deals, we actually got a letter of credit from the bank for 5% of the down payment.

Don't hesitate to ask the seller to finance a portion of the down payment if you want to get into a deal by using less money.

GROSS RENT MULTIPLIER (GRM)

This is a quick way to estimate value, but it isn't very accurate. We use it as a simple tool to see if the property is priced close to the market. If the property seems way overpriced according to this calculation, then we move on and analyze another property.

Example: If a property sells for $1,000,000 and the gross income is $100,000, then the GRM is 10.

$$\frac{Market\ Value}{Gross\ Income}$$

PRICE PER UNIT

We try to get a general idea of what one, two, and three-bedroom units are selling for in a given market to determine the price per unit. This calculation is quick to do, but neglects to take into account several factors, such as square feet, amenities, and income.

$$Price\ Per\ Unit = \frac{Price}{Number\ of\ Units}$$

INCOME PER UNIT

To get the income per unit, divide the GSI by the number of units.

Example: A property with 10 units and $100,000 in GSI has an income of $10,000 per unit.

$$Income\ Per\ Unit = \frac{Gross\ Scheduled\ Income}{Number\ of\ Units}$$

EXPENSES PER UNIT

When evaluating a property, you need to ask appraisers, "What is the typical expense per unit per year?" That will give you a gauge in terms of how much it will cost to run your property per month. When you're about to buy a property, you need to know how much it's going to cost to run it. To calculate the expenses per unit, divide the operating expenses by the number of units.

Example: If a 40-unit property has $80,000 in expenses, then the expenses per unit are $2,000.

$$Expenses\ Per\ Unit = \frac{Operating\ Expenses}{Number\ of\ Units}$$

BREAK-EVEN OCCUPANCY

This calculation will tell you how many units will have to be rented to operate the property and break even. It's extremely helpful when you're repositioning a property with a pre-existing high vacancy rate. You'll get an idea of how many units you're going to need to rent out in order to reach that crucial break-even point.

To calculate this figure, start by dividing the total annual expenses of the property (including debt service) by 12 so you can get a monthly figure. Then, calculate the average rent you receive monthly on the property by adding up all the rent and dividing it by the number of units. Take the figure for monthly expenses and divide it by the average rent, then round up your answer to receive the total units needed to break even. To calculate the percentage of occupancy, take the break-even units and divide by the total units.

Example: Our property at Hickory has 36 units and our annual expenses are $114,000. Divide $114,000 by 12 and the monthly figure is $9,500. The average rent we collect is $390 per apartment. We divide $9,500 by $390 and get 24.35. Therefore, we need 25 units rented to break even. To get the percentage of occupancy, divide 25 units by 36 units for a total of 69% occupancy.

There are several formulas involved in this. They are as follows:

$$Monthly\ Expenses = \frac{Total\ Annual\ Expense}{12}$$

$$Average\ Month\ Rent = \frac{Total\ Monthly\ Rent\ Collected}{Number\ of\ Units}$$

$$Break\ Even\ Occupancy = \frac{Monthly\ Expense}{Average\ Monthly\ Rent}$$

$$Percent\ Occupancy = \frac{Number\ of\ Break\ Even\ Units}{Total\ Units}$$

I know all this can seem overwhelming at first, but keep in mind that we have software available that will help you with the calculations.

INCOME STATEMENT SHEET (FULL INCOME STATEMENT ON PAGE 148)

On the next page is a short cheat sheet for income statements.

Operating Expenses:

Management	
Utilities	
Advertising and Marketing	
Property and Payroll Taxes	
Insurance	
Payroll	
Repairs and Maintenance	
Professional Fees	
Supplies	
Broker Commissions	
Travel Expenses	
Landscaping	
Pest Control	
Permits/Fees	
Snow Removal	
Total Operating Expenses:	

Chapter 6 Summary

Speaking the Language

1. NOI

$$\frac{\text{Gross Operating Income} - \text{Operating Expenses}}{\text{Net Operating Income}}$$

2. Cap Rate

$$\frac{NOI}{\text{Value (Sales Price)}}$$

3. Cash on Cash

$$\frac{\text{Cash Flow}}{\text{Total Cash Invested}}$$

Time for Action

1. What cap rates are units trading for in your market?

2. Based on the cap rates in your market, what type of cash on cash returns can you expect from your next investment?

3. Practice discussing deals with people that you are comfortable with. This is a good way to practice before you engage brokers and bankers.

Check out www.jakeandgino.com for more wealth building tips

Chapter 7

Buy Right
The First Leg of our Wheelbarrow Investment Strategy

*"More money has been made in real estate
than in all industrial investments combined."*

— Andrew Carnegie

To function properly, a wheelbarrow must have three supportive elements: two legs and a wheel. Similarly, our investing system also has three principles that are crucial to its success: **buy right**, **manage right**, and **finance right**.

The first leg of the system is to **buy right**. This is vital above all the others because if you don't buy the property right, the other elements won't save you. On the flip-side, if you buy right, you may be able to overcome pitfalls in poor management or unfavorable financing terms.

What does "buy right" mean?

We buy underperforming apartments known as "mom-and-pop apartments" and reposition them into professionally run, high-performing assets. Our rule of thumb when buying right is to purchase a property that will produce a 10% cash-on-cash return from day one, a figure we arrive at by utilizing the seller's current actual income and our estimated expense costs. Before we buy, we always perform extensive due diligence to gauge how much we'll spend annually on the property expenses.

We begin by researching the seller's tax returns, utility bills, service providers, and any other data they provide. It's vital to base your analysis on the actual numbers instead of proforma data, otherwise you won't have a clear picture of the investment.

Next, we run through these numbers with our team members and create a sample budget for the property. Depending on your market, you can look at different figures to estimate how much expenses are going to be. However, you can typically expect that 50% of the income from the property is going to go towards expenses.

Certain markets will look at costs per unit. In Knoxville, a good rule of thumb for expenses is to expect $3,500 per unit, per year. However, you should only use these to get a quick idea of the operations, as the actual expense cost will vary.

It might seem pointless to create a budget for a property you don't even have yet, but this can allow you to go into the purchase with a clear goal.

Now it's time to verify the annual income of the property by reviewing the seller's taxes from the prior year. The "two percent rule," a useful tool when considering this particular metric, has become popular in recent years. This rule states that to make a good profit on a multifamily investment, the gross monthly rents should be at least two percent of the total purchase price of the property. For example, if you collect $20,000 a month in rent on an investment that costs $1,000,000, you would make a good profit.

The final set of data, a term sheet from the bank, can be gathered now. This is a non-binding agreement that outlines the terms and conditions of the loan. Once we have the sample budget, the verified income, and the terms, we plug these three data sets into our deal analyzer to find out what our offer price will be.

Remember that the seller doesn't typically accept the first offer, so make sure the offer price is about 10% lower than what you're aiming for. If you offer less, the chances of closing the deal on your strike price increases. The great thing about this strategy is that you're making a 10% return from day one, but since you purchased an underperforming mom-and-pop property, you have an excellent opportunity to bump your cash-on-cash return up to 20% or more!

WHAT IS A MOM-AND-POP PROPERTY?

We refer to a property that is being run by an individual, resident manager, or family, instead of by a professional management company, as a mom-and-pop property. Systems are usually nonexistent in these properties, and the landlord is doing all the work. There's no website, and advertising is minimal. It's common for the owner to pay all of the utilities instead of implementing RUBS (Ratio Utility Billing System). There's deferred maintenance, and vacancy tends to be high because the landlord is reluctant to invest back into the property and make repairs. The landlord doesn't charge fees, such as late fees or pet fees, and isn't aggressive about collecting the lower-than-normal rents in a timely fashion. Odds are good that, due to all the stress, the landlord is close to burning out, and it probably shows.

As you will soon find out, we look for ways to increase the value of our properties. If the property is already running smoothly and requires little improvement, the upside for the investor to add value is small. The key to increasing value in any business, especially real estate, is to solve a problem, and the real opportunity lies in being able to identify underperforming assets. If you get this part right, you'll be able to duplicate a similar business plan time and time again.

Arguably, the most important aspect to look for in a property is a motivated seller. It will take some detective work, but it's key to find out early in the process why the property is for sale. Some typical reasons that differentiate standard sellers from motivated sellers are financial problems, burnt-out landlord, deferred maintenance, or personal family disputes.

A motivated seller is one who needs to sell quickly for one of the following reasons:

- Divorce

- Partner Acrimony

- Bankruptcy

- Burned-out Landlord

- Inherited Property

- Retirement

- Bad Health

- New Opportunity

- Relocation

- Code Violations

Earning a 10% cash-on-cash return a must-have metric from day one is a good place to start. It allows you to buy right and have future revenue generators or ways to reduce expenses in order to earn big bucks!

UNDERMANAGED PROPERTIES

Once you've found a mom-and-pop property with a motivated seller, it's time to look into how the property is being managed.

Check to see how involved the owner is in the day-to-day operations and don't hesitate to ask for details regarding the property. Asking the following questions, to yourself or the landlord, is a great place to start:

- Do they manage the property?

- How do they find prospective tenants?

- Are they doing repairs themselves?

- Do they pay the utilities or have a RUBS system in place?

- Do they market the property or have a website?

- How do they collect rent?

- How marketable are the apartment designs?

- Do they have any systems in place such as eviction protocol, rent collection, or property management software?

- Do they utilize software to stay organized?

- Do the apartments have a modern look?

The aforementioned questions will help point you in the right direction. Remember, we're buying failing businesses and turning them into well-oiled machines.

HIGH VACANCY RATES

Just because a property has a high vacancy rate doesn't mean you should shy away from it. Think **opportunity**. Some investors see high vacancy rates and believe it's a product of the location or that the property itself is undesirable. What we find in most of our mom-and-pop acquisitions is that the high vacancy rate is tied directly back to poor management from the owners, and usually for the following reasons:

- **Low web presence:** No website, no internet marketing, no search engine optimization

- **Deferred cosmetic maintenance:** A simple power wash, new mulch, weed killer, or new coat of paint can often fix this.

- **Unrealistic credit expectations for prospective tenants:** If your rent is $600 per month, you may not be able to find tenants with credit scores of 800 and above.

- **Poor maintenance**

- **Poor leasing agents**

- **Owners scaring off prospective tenants with strange rules:** We have seen leases that are 30 pages long.

We believe in value-for-value. If you provide your tenant with a safe, clean, and well-maintained living environment, they'll be more willing to pay few extra bucks in rent.

DEFERRED MAINTENANCE

Poor landscaping is the quickest way to scare off a prospective tenant. In every one of our mom-and-pop acquisitions, we've had to address deferred exterior maintenance. From rusty, mustard yellow doors and shutters to rickety old mailboxes, missing stairs, blasted parking lots, non-working septic systems, broken windows, non-existent flooring, infestations, missing ovens, we've seen it all.

Most exterior deferred maintenance doesn't break the bank, yet it makes a huge difference when showing a property. Increased curb appeal means an increased occupancy rate. The reason we look for this trait is because it's usually a sign of burnt out mom-and-pop owners who are ready to throw in the towel. One of our acquisitions wasn't even on the market, but we noticed exterior deferred maintenance and heard that the family was burnt out, so we made an offer and negotiated a deal.

RENTS BELOW MARKET RATE

A lot of mom-and-pop owners feel like they can't raise their rents to match the market rate. They'll say, "There's a reason those rents are where they are. Don't you think if I could have gotten an extra $100 per month, per unit, I would have by now?" This mindset is one of the defining traits of a mom-and-pop apartment and probably the most lucrative to you.

During your due diligence, you need to ask your broker what the market rent is in your area. Understanding market rent will give you a good idea of what you'll be able to charge for the vacant units when you take over. Have the broker run a Comparative Market Analysis (CMA) of the rents in the area, and compare to your property. Or jump on rentometer.com and to perform your own CMA.

Remember, mom-and-pop owners are typically burned out and don't want to rock the boat. If they have a high vacancy rate and tenants who are paying way below market rent, they're not going to implement a rent increase for fear of losing the tenants they already have. However, this method is like a cancer to your bottom line. If you're not getting enough in rent, you won't have enough to make repairs, and if you don't have enough to make repairs, your property is going to be unattractive to potential new renters. It's a vicious cycle that results in a slow death of your investment.

HIGH EXPENSES

High expenses are an indication of inexperienced managers, and can be a huge negotiating tool. Even though you will be cutting down on day-to-day expenses when you purchase the property, the current expenses influence the overall value of the property. The offer you place on the property is based on the current expenses, not what you speculate in the future. Therefore, the higher the owner's expenses, the lower your purchase price. Below is a short list of where you might be able to reduce costs.

1. **Payroll:** You won't always cut payroll. However, there have been instances where we have reduced payroll costs up to 30%.

2. **Trash Removal:** We have saved thousands negotiating our trash removal with different companies. Our average cost per unit is around $5.50. We have found that most of our sellers were paying upwards of $17.00 per unit. It takes some negotiating and a good relationship with your local rep, but it's worth the time.

3. **Office Phones:** Most properties will have a landline that will cost upwards of $800 - $1,000 per year. In contrast, an unlimited pre-paid cell phone plan could cost about $45 per month and work just fine for you. We typically employ area property managers and this allows them the flexibility to answer the phone from anywhere they are during the day.

4. **Internet and Phone:** Depending on the size of your complex, you might have the option of negotiating for free phone and

Internet for your managers office. We have done this by offering an exclusivity agreement to the cable company.

5. **Advertising:** We have seen a lot of money wasted on the Yellow Pages and local rent magazines. If you're looking to get your name out there, Craigslist is a great free place to start. It's also free and easy to set up a Facebook page for more Internet presence. If you have a large under-rented complex, consider paying for search engine optimization (SEO) from your web development company for the first year until you fill your units.

6. **Services:** At the end of the day, you need to be getting multiple bids for each job and constantly reviewing what you are paying to service providers. This includes insurance, office expenses, pest control, and the list goes on.

THINGS TO LOOK FOR IN A PROPERTY

There are specific things to look for when choosing the right property. Here's a quick list:

- Repairs that need to be done

- Poor management

- Low rents that can be raised

- High expenses that can be reduced through proper management

- A high property vacancy rate

- A burned-out landlord

- Motivated sellers

There are certain aspects of a property that can't or shouldn't be fixed. If the necessary repairs are too extensive or require a major overhaul, don't buy. Here's a list of deal breakers:

- Structural problems (cracked foundation, etc.)

- Environmental issues (high rates of flooding, fault lines, mudslides)

- High vacancy rates in market or over-saturation of apartments

- Lack of nearby amenities (supermarkets, transportation, jobs)

On the flip side, there are aspects that you should keep an eye out for that could be a sign you've found a good investment property:

- Low rental rates as compared to market rents

- Deferred maintenance, such as messy landscaping and peeling paint

- No RUBS program

- Lack of income from pets, laundry, storage, vending, parking, etc.

- Garages/Storage units that tenants can use

SIZE DOESN'T MATTER

Some get the impression that the definition of a mom-and-pop multi-family property is limited to a 2-10 unit apartment complex. The truth is that mom-and-pops come in all shapes and sizes. For example, the ones we've invested in range in size from 25 to 280 units, but they all had the same opportunities: deferred maintenance, poor management, and high vacancies. The point here is that "mom-and-pop" has little to do with size and everything to do with giving you the chance to buy underperforming properties and reposition them. If you were to buy an investment property that was already repositioned, most of the value adds will already be taken care of, thus leaving you with little-to-no room to increase revenue and decrease expenses.

Do Your Due Diligence

There are several issues that can be identified during the due diligence phase:

1. Repair costs/larger capital improvement too high

2. Poor tenancy with low security deposits

3. Leases don't match lease schedule

4. Run out of time

5. Property owner isn't cooperative

Underestimating repair costs is a common mistake that's made during the inspection of the property. When you have an inspector check the property, he'll present you with a detailed report that lists all the defects and repairs that will need to be performed. Make sure he gets into every unit or else the inspection is incomplete.

When we inspected one of our properties, the inspector noted that the roof and siding on one of the structures needed to be replaced. We went back to the sellers and showed them the inspection report, and the solution was for them to replace the roof and siding before we took possession of the property. We had the option to ask for a repair allowance at closing and fix it ourselves, however, we found it easier in this situation to have the sellers perform the repairs because they already had a construction crew.

Here is an After Repair Value List that we use to analyze how much money it will cost to renovate a property. We list each item individually, then figure out how much each item will cost. For example, a 30-yard garbage dumpster in our market costs approximately $600. If we need 2 dumpsters, then we allocate $1,200 for dumpsters in our analysis. This gives us a pretty accurate estimate on our renovation costs.

Apartment Turn Calculator
After Repair Value - Cost-Profit = Buy Price

Prices will vary from market to market

Item	Unit	Cost	Quantity	Total
Demo	Hrs	$30.00	1	$ 30.00
Dumpster	amount	$500.00		$ -
Landscaping	Hrs	$30.00		$ -
Mulch	yard	$35.00		$ -
Roof	square	$130.00		$ -
Plywood	amount	$50.00		$ -
Windows	amount	$220.00		$ -
Gutters	linear ft	$2.50		$ -
Exterior Door	amount	$250.00		$ -
Lockset	amount	$60.00		$ -
Storm Door	amount	$150.00		$ -
Garage Door	amount	$500.00		$ -
Vinyl Siding	square	$200.00		$ -
Paint Exterior	square ft	$1.00		$ -
A/C 4 ton installed	amount	$2,200.00		$ -
Kitchen cabinets				
2 bed apartment	material	$1,200.00		$ -
	labor	$300.00		$ -
Formica	sq ft	$10.00		$ -
Backsplash	sq ft	$10.00		$ -
Stove/dishwasher/micro		$900.00		$ -
Fridge	amt	$400.00		$ -
Flooring Combo	sq ft	$1.35		$ -
Bathroom 5X7 size				
tub	amount	$160.00		$ -
toilet	amount	$150.00		$ -
fixtures	amount	$190.00		$ -
vanity sink	amount	$160.00		$ -
accesor	amount	$200.00		$ -
misc	amount	$200.00		$ -
Drywall	sq ft	$1.00		$ -
labor & material				
Repair	Hrs	$30.00		$ -
Paint interior	sq ft	$1.00		$ -
Doors/trim	sq ft	$1.50		$ -
Doors	amount	$100.00		$ -
Bifold closet 2x36	amount	$120.00		$ -
Water HTR	amount	$550.00		$ -
water htr 40 gall				
Pex	sq ft	$1.00		$ -
Laundrytub/faucet	amount	$175.00		$ -
Mechanical				
Heating unit	amount	$2,500.00		$ -
ductwork	amount	$500.00		$ -
Electrrical	sq ft	$1.75		$ -
100 amp breaker box	amount	$475.00		$ -
Meter box/cable	amount	$425.00		$ -
Hardwire smokes	amount	$60.00		$ -
Plugs/switches	amount	$15.00		$ -
GFI	amount	$20.00		$ -
Light Fixtures	amount	$10.00		$ -
Permits		$0.00		$ -
Cleaning		$0.00		$ -
Add Rows				$ -
Utilities per month		$35.00		$ -
total				$ 30.00

Taking over a property with sub-par tenants can be a real challenge for landlords. You're inheriting someone else's problems, and that's why you should be buying the property at a discount. Sub-par tenants can be classified in six key ways:

1. Late payers

2. Non-payers

3. Disruptive to the community

4. Destructive to the property

5. Rule breakers

6. Drug crowd

Once you begin repositioning the property, sub-par tenants are usually the first ones to check out. Increasing the rent as soon as their new lease comes up also aids in their departure.

You don't always have to get rid of sub-par tenants. When we took over our first property, we noticed that some of these tenants changed their behavior and became good tenants once we added value to their environment. A good tenant expects (and deserves) quality service and will pay a fair price for it.

During the due diligence phase, the seller will send over a **rent roll audit** that lists all the current leases. This audit should include when the leases begin and end, the monthly rent prices, apartment numbers, names of the tenants, the number of tenants occupying each space, the security deposit amounts (refundable or non-refundable), and if the tenants are paying any additional fees. Your job is to calculate the monthly rental income and make sure it matches the numbers you received from the seller. Banks are very interested in making sure that the property is generating the stated income. Naturally, if the numbers are off you should go back to the seller and either negotiate a lower price or walk away from the deal. It may be difficult to secure financing if the income is much lower than the initial figures that were provided.

Running out of time is another obstacle you might face when trying to close a deal. The simplest way to handle this problem is to have your attorney put extensions into the purchase and sale agreement or state that the contract is contingent on your ability to get financing. Attempting to secure financing is typically the number one cause for deals to extend beyond the closing date. We fell into this trap with our second deal.

We were trying to convince the seller to give us a couple more days for the bank to issue the mortgage, and we were in serious jeopardy of forfeiting our down payment. Luckily, we convinced the seller to extend the closing date by a few days if we gave him back $4,000 of our repair allowance. We breathed a sigh of relief when he agreed to give us the extension. Ironically, the seller was so focused on "winning" that he never bothered prorating the rents at the time of closing. We closed on the 3rd day of the month, and he was entitled to three days worth of rent, but he was only concerned with receiving the allowance money.

Our recommendation is to have a 60-day closing from the day you receive all due diligence documents, and negotiate for two 30-day extensions if needed.

Uncooperative property owners can be a serious drag when you're trying to perform due diligence and close a deal. Our suggestion is for you to request all due diligence documents to be given to you in their entirety and all at once. Do not start the contract time frame until you receive **all** the documents. Some sellers are unorganized and others have something to hide, but this may work to your advantage. If you show persistence, you may unearth a good deal others miss because most buyers will give up when dealing with a difficult seller.

Checklists

Takeover Checklist

There are dozens of actions that have to be executed before taking over a property, and the list below contains all of these steps.

Prior to Takeover (One Month Out)

1. Review your current insurance and get a quote from your insurance broker.

2. Choose property management software.

3. Order computer and office supplies.

4. Prepare takeover letters for tenants.

5. Establish checking accounts at a bank.

6. Create logos and order new marketing materials.

7. Review current contracts for laundry, pests, landscaping, and pool.

8. Contact Laundry Company and negotiate contract if you decide not to manage it yourself.

9. Review the garbage bill and get a new quote.

10. Review the utility usage.

11. Schedule phone and internet service.

12. Get a copy of the budget, rehab budget, and proforma.

13. Contact RUBS company and begin to gather all tenant data.

14. Review the current employees and decide if you're going to retain them.

15. Begin to interview potential employees.

16. Set up payroll service (we use ADP).

17. Get quotes for any repairs discovered during the inspection.

18. Set up Home Depot/Lowes accounts.

19. Review copies of any litigation and tenant evictions.

20. Interview management companies.

21. Obtain a list of personal property, including appliances, equipment, and supplies.

22. Get list of outstanding maintenance requests.

Day of Takeover

1. Inspect all units for carpeting, appliances, and smoke detectors.

2. Deliver resident takeover letters.

3. Begin to institute RUBS.

4. Address outstanding maintenance requests.

5. Begin implementing newly acquired vendor services for the pool, landscaping, cable, elevator, etc.

6. Order business cards for staff.

7. Have a locksmith change the locks to the office, common areas, and maintenance shop.

8. Set up an answering machine and call center if you use this service.

9. Confirm that the utility service is transferred into your name.

CHAPTER 7 SUMMARY

Buy Right

1. Find the highly motivated mom-and-pop apartment owners.

2. Buy on actual numbers, no rosy pro-formas. We shoot for 10% cash on cash returns and 8% cap rates.

3. Be thorough during due diligence. We ask for 100% rent ready units.

Time for action

1. Have you identified any motivated sellers?

2. Are you comfortable enough analyzing deals to buy on actuals?

3. How many offers have you made this month?

Check out www.jakeandgino.com for more wealth building tips

Chapter 8

Manage Right
The "Wheel" of the Wheelbarrow Profits Framework

This isn't a "how to" chapter on starting a property management company. This chapter lays out our strategies on how to reposition an underperforming mom-and-pop apartment complex for big bucks. We don't run our properties personally; we've built up a property management company to run the day-to-day operations for us. If you don't envision yourself building a property management company, that's okay. You can hire a company and have them follow our steps.

How to Reposition a Mom-and-Pop Apartment Complex
– Three Steps to 30% Cash-on-Cash Returns –

Before we begin, remember that not every mom-and-pop apartment complex is the same. However, we've developed a proven strategy that fits the bill for most. Our strategy works best with mom-and-pop owners who have high vacancy rates, deferred maintenance, no RUBS system in place, rents below market rates, and high expenses.

Each deal will be different. You may be able to negotiate a repair allowance that's paid to you at closing depending on the situation. For example, your inspector may find that two of the units are completely gutted. Keep in mind that the negotiation for such additional considerations must take place prior to closing.

Once the property is sold, one thing you can count on is that your tenants are going to worry about their rent going up. Before you attempt to raise tenant costs, you should start your renovations. There's a couple of reasons for this: chief among them is that you very well might lose residents due to increased rent, and you're going to need an uninterrupted revenue stream to help you pay for your renovations. The second reason is that your tenants might see that your renovations are changing their complex for the better, and those who were previously thinking about leaving for fear of having to pay more each month might now think that it's worth it to stay.

Repositioning a property isn't just about making money. It's about treating tenants well, giving them a safe place to stay, and making them feel as though they're getting their money's worth. The more tenants feel like they're getting value for value, the more likely they are to stay and even tell their friends when an apartment becomes available.

WHEELBARROW PROFITS REPOSITIONING FRAMEWORK

Before you even get started, it's important to know what the difference is between an improvement and a repair. **Repairs** are done to fix and maintain a property, while an **improvement** is something that adds value to your property. In regards to the IRS, repairs are considered expenses in the year in which they were made, while an improvement is depreciated.

Repairs include:	Improvements include:
Fixing broken windows	Adding an addition onto the complex
Replacing shingles	Installing a pool
Fixing a broken stove	Installing a garage
Replacing a carbon monoxide detector	Replacing the entire roof
Painting a room	Installing a security system
Replacing a cracked shower tile	Installing central air
Fixing lights that don't turn on	Renovating several bathrooms
Fixing a broken doorknob	Adding a new plumbing system
Fixing toilets that don't flush	Installing all new electrical wiring

When repositioning, you'll need to balance both to bring added value, and profits, to your investment.

STEP 1: FILL THE VACANT UNITS AT MARKET RENTS
*MASSIVE REVENUE GENERATOR #1

We typically have a 20-30% vacancy rate on the day of takeover. Our first step is to transform the vacant units with our modern paint scheme and renovations. We immediately post these pictures online and begin filling the vacant units. Our "modern affordability" offer includes two-tone paint schemes, updated flooring, new fixtures, and we may paint the cabinets. These simple upgrades make all the difference in the world when it comes to renting apartments. Our exterior upgrades such as shutters, paint, and landscaping will begin at the same time. Our team has been able to fill 30 vacant units within 60 days by utilizing this strategy. It's amazing what can happen when a community believes in your vision. We get many tenants asking us "When is my breezeway getting painted?" or "When will my building get shutters?" These are the types of conversations you want to be having with your residents.

When you begin to reposition, its important to ask yourself which renovations are going get the most bang for your buck by lowering costs and which ones are going to draw in more tenants. You can't charge market rent prices and not make the appropriate changes unless there's a shortage of apartments in that market. It's pride of ownership for our group. We take pride in creating clean, safe, and affordable communities.

One of the easiest ways that you can immediately improve a property is by tackling the outside. Yes, tenants are going to be living in the units, but they have to want to get there first. If a prospective tenant drives by and sees a run down building with overgrown landscaping and garbage everywhere, what do you think the chances are that they're even going to get out of the car to see what the inside looks like?

The best part is that the exterior improvements are simple and relatively inexpensive, and once they're finished they start drawing in potential new tenants right away. Some of the simple but powerful changes you can make include:

1. Fixing damaged fencing

2. Adding new outdoor lighting

3. Adding flowers

4. Replacing railings

5. Adding benches

6. Replacing outdated mailboxes

7. Trimming down the hedges

8. Trimming hanging tree branches

9. Putting in new doors

10. Adding fencing around garbage dumpsters

11. Power-washing the facade

12. Repainting the facade

13. Adding a new sign

We start the exterior upgrades while renovating and filling the vacant units. Your first step should be taking on the vacant units. Why start with them first? When they're empty, they're not making money. The sooner they're up-and-running, the more quickly they can start generating revenue. Replace anything that's damaged or outdated, and make sure to have the plumbing and electrical inspected to ensure it's all in working order.

Keep in mind that the two most important rooms of the unit are the kitchen and the bathroom, so you'll want to focus the majority of your efforts here. We'll make several changes in the kitchen, such as replacing countertops, fixing leaky faucets, getting new appliances, and repainting kitchen cabinets. In the bathroom we'll add new grouting, fix any cracked tiles, and update the sinks and vanity if they're outdated.

Once the interiors of the vacant units are finished, you'll also want to make sure to take care of the common areas, such as the laundry room and hallway. You'll hear us mention a few times about how beneficial it is to contract out the laundry room and how we do so with a company called Coinmach. It's one less thing we have to worry about. They provide us with and maintain the machines, we split the revenue, and that's all there is to it. Owners of mom-and-pop apartment complexes typically start out trying to do everything themselves, but that's going to be their downfall. Sometimes you just have to delegate, and if you can do so and earn money in the process, why not?

For the hallway, you can add a fresh coat of paint, replace any outdated light fixtures, make sure the flooring isn't damaged, check that the windows are clean and in good condition, and install new smoke detectors if they're not currently in working order. The hallways may not seem important, but your tenants will have to walk through them every day. You should consider the hallways of your property an extension of their home, where they have the right to feel and be safe.

Step 2. Implement RUBS
*Massive Revenue Generator # 2

We've mentioned RUBS a few times throughout this book, but now it's time to flip the switch. You can use RUBS for almost all of the utilities that are offered, from gas to trash. You recoup the utility bills by billing the utilities back to the tenant, so it's a lot less you have to worry about.

All of your new tenants will be added to the RUBS program but you must also add any tenants with expired leases. It typically takes 6–12 months to get every tenant on the RUBS program, so start early.

STEP 3. RAISE THE REMAINING TENANTS TO MARKET RENTS
*MASSIVE REVENUE GENERATOR #3

Now that you've filled the vacant units at market rents and implemented the RUBS program, it's time to raise the remaining renters to market rate prices. Don't be one of the mom-and-pop apartment complex owners who skips on doing this because they're scared of losing tenants. After all the changes you've made, you deserve to raise the rent prices to a number that's in line with the rest of the marketplace. As long as you offer quality units at market rent prices, there will always be tenants who are willing to live there and pay what you ask. Once we have stabilized the complex, we begin this process. If we have forty units that are under market, we may start by raising eight units per month to test the water. If we lose all eight, we may pull back to four the next month, until the process is complete.

Recap of the WBP repositioning framework

1. Fill the vacant units at market rents

2. Implement RUBS

3. Raise the remaining tenants to market rents

STEP 3.1 BE CONSISTENT WITH MAINTAINING YOUR PROPERTY

You don't want to reposition the mom-and-pop property just to make money in the short term. It's important to think about the potential for long-term cash flow, and the best way to do that is to be consistent through your care of your tenants and the management of the property.

Making changes to the property is not a one-and-done project; it's a long-term commitment.

It's a good idea to hold mandatory meetings as often as you deem necessary so you can ensure that your entire team is on the same page. You can discuss ways to make even more improvements, go over any tenant issues that have come up, and talk about how you can keep the complex moving in a positive direction.

Don't just talk about keeping the property in good shape. You have to actually ensure it happens. This involves handling any issues in a timely manner, constantly keeping the property in good condition, and letting your tenants know that you're committed to providing them with a safe place to live.

Here are our 21 reasons to maintain your property.

1. It maintains the value of the asset and its resale value.

2. It allows you to increase rents.

3. It minimizes tenant turnover.

4. Happy and satisfied tenants stay in one place longer.

5. The expenses of the property are reduced.

6. It allows you to rent out the apartments more easily.

7. Turning a vacant apartment will allow you to rent quicker.

8. You attract better quality tenants.

9. There's less of a chance of an accident occurring on the property.

10. More insurance companies will be willing to insure the property.

11. Your insurance rates will be lower.

12. You're less likely to have a problem with collecting an insurance claim on the property if everything is running, as it should.

13. It reduces problems that just pop up (i.e. a clogged line).

14. It allows for better control of the property.

15. It's easier to secure financing.

16. Tenants follow your lead and take care of the property.

17. You have a better relationship with town officials.

18. You incur no fines from the local or county government for violations.

19. You develop a sense of pride in owning a nice asset and offering good, safe housing.

20. It helps raise the value of the entire neighborhood.

21. It saves time on repairs. Maintenance is less work.

OUR TOP MOM-AND-POP VALUE PLAYS

When you're repositioning a property it's easy to get overwhelmed with all the possible changes that you can make. It's a lot to take on, but there are certain big value plays that you should make first so you can make the most of your purchase and get the best results.

PAINT

The quickest way to class up an older property is with a fresh coat of paint inside and out. Since most of our apartment buildings are brick, we like to paint the doors and shutters with a semi-gloss black. This immediately creates a classy look. You may have stairways or decks that need a fresh coat of paint as well.

We've had good success with two-tone color schemes inside apartments. For example, we tend to go with a white semi-gloss for the baseboards and a light gray or beige for the walls. It sounds simple, but it will help your property stand out, especially when most apartments paint their walls and trim a basic white.

Don't delay. This is the first sign to your tenants that positive changes are on the way.

LANDSCAPING/PRESSURE WASH

These two items go hand-in-hand during the immediate repositioning phase. Pressure washing almost always needs to be done on the decks, stairways, and any vinyl siding. We have some buildings with vinyl siding, and you can always see a huge difference after they're pressure washed. After the building is clean, we like to make sure the bushes are pruned and that fresh mulch is added. Sometimes, we'll add new low maintenance decorative trees if we believe it will make a big impact on the curb appeal. This isn't rocket science, but all of this is almost always left unattended with mom-and-pop apartments.

COINMACH / SELL OLD LAUNDRY MACHINES

The laundry room is often a neglected area of a mom-and-pop apartment complex, not just because the machines are expensive to fix but because maintenance employees have to devote a lot of time to them when they also have other things to do. It's a good idea to contract the washers and dryers out to a service company like Coinmach. They typically pay us a 60-40 split on the gross laundry revenue and will also pay you six months of the projected gross upfront revenue for signing a contract. Additionally, they provide all of the washers and dryers as well as offer free maintenance. The payments, plus the sale of your old machines, are a nice immediate addition to your capital expenditures. This service allows us to focus our attention on other areas and still profit from the laundry service.

IMPLEMENTING SEO

It's a good idea to implement SEO (Search Engine Optimization) tactics on your website. This will keep your website at the top of search results when potential tenants are looking for apartments. Don't underestimate the power of SEO. It can mean the difference between you ending up on the first page of search results with several interested tenants calling you every day and being located several pages back where hardly anyone will see you.

How to Make Money Screening for Tenants

We charge $40 to screen our tenants, but the actual cost for the screening is $16. Therefore, every time a tenant applies we make $24. Depending on the size of the property, we've made between $300-$500 per month on application fees alone. Our screening service is national and offered through our software company. Many apartment complexes charge even more for application fees, so there's potential room for growth here.

The other way to make money is by selecting quality tenants. If someone has been evicted before, he'll probably take his chances again in the future. We'll never rent to someone who has a prior eviction. The point here is that you make money the longer you can keep a good tenant and not have to "turn" an apartment. Get the best quality tenant upfront and treat them like gold.

Pet Fees

When we first started in the business we were repositioning properties that had existing policies not allowing pets. However, this significantly limits your potential tenant pool and you're losing out on quite a bit of money.

There's two different ways that you can go about charging pet fees. The first is to charge a large deposit or non-refundable fee of around $500; the second is to charge a non-refundable fee (around $100) and $25-$50 per month per pet. We prefer the second method because it allows more people access to the apartment and gives us a larger return over time.

Move-In Fee vs. Deposit

This is an area where many seasoned investors would disagree with our strategy. Let's compare the two and then tell you why we do what we do.

When you collect a deposit, you place the amount you charge into an interest bearing bank account and pay the tenant the interest earned every year. At the end of their tenancy, you evaluate the condition of the apartment and reimburse the tenant their owed deposit amount.

Conversely, we charge a non-refundable "move-in fee." There's no bank account to set up, no deposit to reimburse, and all the money collected stays with us. We do, however, charge for excessive damages.

Now, the reason we collect the move-in fee instead of a deposit is because in our area, where we have B-/C+ apartments, deposits range from $250-$500. Currently, we charge a $400 move-in fee. We don't get pushback from tenants on this and can avoid the administrative work of the deposit. Collecting a move-in fee also allows us to keep the entire amount regardless of unit's condition.

MAINTENANCE

Remember: Good maintenance = long-term tenant = low turnover costs. Highly skilled maintenance support can be hard to find, but they do exist, so don't just settle for a team or individual that is sub-par. One of the biggest downfalls of a mom-and-pop complex tends to be a lack of, or deferred, maintenance. Some say that the magic number is one maintenance employee for every 75-100 units. This ratio all depends on how you define maintenance work and how efficient your maintenance team is. The key is to not let tenant issues build up or your number of vacancies will follow suite.

You can't expect to charge higher rents if you can't meet your tenant's needs in a timely fashion. Neglecting your tenants and then asking for more money is a recipe for disaster. Remember, we provide value for value. Show your tenants that you provide safe, clean, and efficient living with timely maintenance and they'll stay with you through the rent increases.

WHAT TO FIX

We've already discussed what repairs and improvements are best for a mom-and-pop complex from an investment perspective, but there's one other thing you need to do when you're repositioning an apartment: think like a tenant.

Providing a clean and safe place for your tenants to live is obviously important, but there's more to it than that. Start off repositioning the property like an owner, but finish looking at it like a tenant. Before you put your stamp of approval on everything, walk around and examine it as if you were a tenant doing a tour of the property and unit. Look at things that they would look at and think like they would.

For example, if you're a tenant and have the option to store your belongings in a garage on the property, but the garage is in horrible shape, are you going to pay your hard-earned money to leave your possessions there? No, you're going to go to the nearest storage unit instead where your things will be clean and safe. As an owner, everything on the property is an extension of each individual unit, which means it should also be well cared for and in good condition. If you have storage spaces on the property, clean them out so your tenants have somewhere to store their extra items. The benefit is that you can charge a rental fee in the process. Remember, value for value is our motto. Plus, when tenants have a place to store all their extras, they're less likely to move to find a larger space that will accommodate all the items they have.

If you want a second opinion on the tenant's perspective, call in a neutral party whose opinion you value and ask them to walk around with a clipboard and make notes of everything they noticed. They might be big things or little things, but at least you can get them taken care of before an actual potential tenant notices them first.

Our repositioning framework is going to make it easy to get everything done in an effective and orderly fashion. The more often you do it, the easier it gets. After awhile it will all seem like second nature, and you'll be well on your way to earning the money you desire by turning mom-and-pop apartments into well oiled machines.

CHAPTER 8 SUMMARY

MANAGE RIGHT

1.) Fill the vacant units at market rents.

2.) Implement RUBS.

3.) Raise the remaining tenants to market rents.

TIME FOR ACTION

1.) What is the market rent for your units?

2.) Have you established a relationship with a RUBS company yet?

3.) Do you have the right team in place to ensure a proper reposition?

Check out www.jakeandgino.com for more wealth building tips

CHAPTER 9

FINANCE RIGHT
THE THIRD PILLAR OF OUR
WHEELBARROW STRATEGY

The hardest part of buying multifamily apartments is negotiating a favorable deal with the seller, but negotiating terms with the bank is a close second. The bank will be quick to give you their terms for amortization, interest rate, and the percent down or down payment. Your job is to root out what the going rates are and then find a bank willing to give you a better deal. Per transaction, we will get terms from an average of 3-5 banks. This takes time, but never fails to get us the best possible deal.

To speed up our deals, we will typically utilize local lenders as "bridge loans." This works by taking out a mortgage from a local lender with the intention of refinancing the loan within three years. Since the properties we buy are underperforming, our preferred lenders will not loan to us until we have repositioned the property to a favorable investment.

It's important to note, these are not true bridge loans. We view them as bridge loans because it is our goal to secure a non-recourse loan within three years. Because you will be refinancing within a short period, it's key to negotiate a low prepayment penalty on this loan.

Your next step, when the time is right, would be to secure that non-recourse loan. This is a loan that is secured by real property, but the borrower is not personally liable. The bottom line here is, if you default, the bank can take the apartments but cannot come after your personal assets.

Fannie/Freddie, FHA, insurance companies, and CMBS (collateralized mortgage backed securities) all have non-recourse loan options. You will hear this referred to as the "secondary market."

STRATEGY OUTLINE

1. Secure underperforming property with a local lender. This acts as your "bridge" loan.

2. Reposition the property to make it more desirable for the secondary market.

3. Refinance to a non-recourse loan.

WHY IS THIS A GREAT STRATEGY?

We have had success with this strategy for a few reasons. First, the refi to non-recourse takes the property off of our personal balance sheets, thus eliminating our risk. Secondly, we are typically able to pull money out of the refi tax-free. You see, if our initial recourse loan was $3,450,000 we could get a new non-recourse loan for around $4,500,000. We can use the additional funds to create more improvements, upping the value of the property. Also, the secondary market offers lower rates and longer amortization so we can do all this without disrupting our monthly revenue.

We're able to control how much our property is worth through forced appreciation by buying right and managing right. This is key because we don't wait for the market to rise. We increase the net income thus making the property worth more. Since our properties generate a great deal of additional income after the reposition, appraisers will apply a higher valuation since they primarily utilize the income approach for multifamily appraisals. We have pulled out over $1.6 million dollars on a single refi utilizing this strategy. Additionally, those extra funds are tax-free until you sell the property. Our model is to buy and hold, so we're not planning to sell anytime soon. One of our partners calls this "investment nirvana" for obvious reasons.

WHAT WILL THE SEASONED INVESTOR TELL YOU?

Most seasoned investors look for three things:

1. Liquidity
2. Leverage
3. Control

Real Estate typically meets the second and third criteria listed above, but falls short on liquidity. This may be a positive for some investors because it deters them from selling the asset too quickly before realizing potential gains. Real estate does allow you to refinance a property and pull out money (tax deferred) when you refinance. Just be cautioned that if you take out a refi, and sell in two years, you'll have to pay taxes on the money you took out. That's why this strategy works best with our buy-and-hold model. If you don't sell, you don't have to pay off the taxes.

WHERE DO YOU FIND THE MONEY FOR THE DOWN PAYMENT?

Now that you've found the deal, where are you going to find the cash for your down payment? Here are several ways to come up with the money.

SAVINGS

This is probably the most obvious avenue to pursue. We have accounts that we call our "Financial Freedom account" where we allocate 10% of all our monthly earnings. The goal is to turn earned income into passive income, so the money that has accumulated in the Financial Freedom account is used solely for investments: stocks, bonds, real estate, and business opportunities.

HOME EQUITY

If you have equity in your home, it may be time to have that equity work for you. Walk into any bank, and apply for a HELOC (home equity line of credit). The only drawback with using an equity loan is that the interest rate is not fixed. We have become accustomed to a low-interest rate environment, but one-day rates will rise again, and our payment will also rise. The idea here is to utilize the extra cash flow from the property to pay down the HELOC in short order.

PARTNERS

We have been fortunate to partner with an extremely savvy and knowledgeable investor in our properties in Tennessee. Partners allow you to purchase larger deals and enhance the partnership's credibility and balance sheet. When choosing a partner, make sure that you share the same vision and investing criteria. It would be a huge problem if Jake liked to flip houses, but Gino's preference was to buy and hold.

FAMILY

Not all of us have a rich uncle, but if you do, show him your business plan and ask if he wants to invest with you. Make sure your family understands, you're not asking for money; you are offering an opportunity to earn a substantial return. Our recommendation is to treat a loan from a family member identically to that of a stranger. Document everything and have a lawyer draw up the appropriate papers. You do not want to have any misunderstandings with family members, especially when money is involved.

CREDIT CARDS

Some investors use their credit cards as a down payment. I would only recommend using credit cards if you are fixing a property and flipping it. The interest rates are onerous, and the cardholder will incur steep penalties if the balance is not paid off. On the other hand, if you need the money for a short time frame, it might be worth it. Make sure to add the additional costs to the ARV (After Repair Value) and to budget for these expenses.

For every property that we purchase, we get a company credit card. This is for any expenses associated with buying the property, and by the time the deal goes through we are able to pay off the card with the proceeds.

LIFE INSURANCE

When Gino purchased his first duplex in Rochester, he borrowed the down payment from the cash value of his life insurance policy. He had decided to purchase whole life years earlier, instead of allocating the resources to an IRA or pension plan. The plan was to access the funds before he turned 59 ½ years old and use it as a forced savings strategy and an estate-planning tool. Purchasing whole life is a long-term strategy and should be carefully considered. The whole life accrues a cash value along with providing a death benefit to the policyholder. Unfortunately, the policies tend to be costly and take several years before noticing an accumulation of cash value. If you purchase the policies at a relatively young age and have patience, you will be rewarded.

Gino was able to use the remaining cash value in the policy as collateral for the down payment on our third investment. The bank required that we deposit an additional $200,000 in escrow, and they would release the funds at the end of 3 years. He was permitted to assign the cash value of the policy over to the bank and save himself the agony of withdrawing from his savings. It was a home run.

SELF-DIRECTED IRA

It was a shock for us to discover that it was possible to utilize an IRA to invest in real estate. We thought that funds held in retirement accounts could only be invested in stocks and bonds. This makes sense, since everyone in the investment community wants investors to maintain their assets in mutual funds. That way, they rely on those expensive fund managers.

When Gino found out that using IRA funds was permissible, he went online to see what companies offered this service. His first step was to set up a self-directed IRA with a custodian. He contacted a company called Equity Trust (www.trustetc.com) and filled out all of the appropriate forms. They have a wealth of information on their website about the rules and regulations of investing with self-directed IRAs. We even signed up for a couple of their webinars. Then he transferred the assets from his pension plan into the custodian account. There are a few rules regarding permissible investments.

To keep it simple, you are not allowed to invest in life insurance, collectibles such as rugs and paintings, and certain coins. These investment options are considered "prohibited transactions." As you can see, your self-directed IRA gives you the ability to control your portfolio and also gives you a variety of different investment vehicles.

Closing at the Beginning of the Month

Some investors prefer to schedule their closings at the beginning of the month, where they're entitled to that month's prepaid rents. If you close on January 2nd the rents are prorated, which means you would be entitled to 29 days of the monthly rent. In some transactions, you can use the prorated rent to decrease the amount of cash needed to close the deal. In our third deal, we requested the prorated rents to be wired into our banking account. This money was used to begin our deferred maintenance repairs.

Hard Money Loans or Investor Loans

You may be putting a deal together with multiple investors that have varying levels of capital to contribute. If this is the case and you have less capital to contribute than other partners, you may consider asking one of the partners to give you a loan for part of the down payment. The terms would be negotiable. This loan could be paid by your cash flow from the new entity. This will enable you to gain more equity in the deal due to the smaller down payment amount. The same can be achieved with hard money loans or lines of credit from a bank.

There Are Several Ways That Your Deal Can Be Financed

Cash

Very few investors can pay all cash for an investment, because few have the funds immediately available to them. Even if you have the means, this isn't the best strategy. When you pay up front, you lose the ability to leverage your investment. One of the biggest benefits of investment properties is that the tenants pay down your mortgage for you.

Mortgage

This is arguably the most common way to finance the acquisition of a property. A mortgage can be originated from a bank or you can obtain the services of a mortgage broker to shop around your investment to acquire a loan.

Lenders

1. **Direct Lenders:** Banks, insurance companies, pension funds, credit unions and REITs fall into this category.

2. **Syndicate Lenders:** These lenders pool money together, and are willing to assume more risk because they are not regulated by any state or federal agency.

3. **Government agencies:** Fannie Mae and Freddie Mac were established to provide local banks with money to help finance mortgages in an attempt to raise home ownership. A secondary market was formed to create greater liquidity. The banks would sell their loans to Fannie and Freddie, and in turn, Fannie and Freddie would pool these loans together and convert them into Collateral Mortgage Backed Securities.

Seller Financing

This technique can be utilized when you are dealing with a motivated seller or someone choosing to defer some of their capital gains. We had the sellers hold a second mortgage on our first deal. The bank gave us a mortgage for 80% of the sale price, and the sellers held a note for 10% of the sales price. This meant that we only had to come up with 10% of the property price for the down payment. We were able to preserve capital to perform improvements to the property and used the remaining capital for a down payment on our second purchase. No money is exchanged. It is a form of credit given to the buyer to help sell the property.

In the beginning, the local banks won't offer you very good terms. That's why your first request from mom-and-pop sellers should always be seller financing. Seller financing terms are very negotiable. In our experience, motivated mom-and-pop sellers will simply want to negotiate term and interest rate. You will also have a better opportunity negotiating favorable terms with a mom-and-pop seller vs. a bank.

We have been told by many people that seller financing doesn't work, or to stop wasting our time. Don't listen to the naysayers! If the seller doesn't want to hold the note for the entire property, maybe they will hold the note for half of the loan amount, or possibly the down payment. Seller financing is very real and very possible.

One strategy that some investors use is to purchase the property with seller financing and then buy back the note at a discount.

Why would the owner sell the note at a discount?

- Divorce

- Note holder wants to buy a luxury or take an expensive vacation

- Pay bills, such as college

- Health reasons

- Loss of employment

- Note holder moves

- Note holder passes away & family wants to sell

- Banks will not finance another endeavor

The notes created for seller financing should be structured with terms favorable to you whenever possible. You should ask for:

- No due on sale clause – the balance of the loan may be called due on the sale or transcript used to secure the note.

- No prepayment penalty

- Long amortization schedule

- Lower interest rates

- No late fee (this is a stretch, but it's still good to ask)

LOAN ASSUMPTION

You would think that assuming a loan would speed up the process, but it usually takes longer to assume an existing loan than getting one on your own. However, there are a few advantages. Closing costs are lower and the interest rate on the assumed loan is often less than the current market rate. Remember that when assuming a loan, you will still need to go through the bank's approval process.

WHAT TO NEGOTIATE

The following are some terms and real-world examples that have shaped the way we negotiate.

NEGOTIATING DOWN PAYMENTS

The benefit to negotiating the down payment is that it allows you to buy a property for less money down. In our experience with banks, we have only been able to negotiate the down payment to 15% of the loan, but you can get creative. Here are some strategies:

1. Ask the current owner to seller finance part of the down payment. This will only be a small note for the seller compared to his sale price. An agreeable scenario may be to have the seller finance 10% of the down payment and you finance the remaining percentage.

2. Have the bank set up an escrow account for 5-10% of the down payment to be released over 36 months. You will then need to get a letter of credit, a line of credit, or borrow the money from a hard moneylender for the escrow account. This escrow will be returned to you. Usually the bank will release the money as follows:

   25% after 12 months
   25% after 24 months
   50% after 36 months

   Like anything, these terms are negotiable.

3. If you are working with partners, you may have a partner who is interested in holding a note for part of the down payment. This is a solid investment because the property will be paying this person and the terms could be written favorably for all parties.

4. Borrow money from your self directed IRA

5. Home equity loan – This is a loan that will allow you to borrow the built up equity you have in your home. If you have been in your home for many years, this may be a good option. These loans are typically variable based on prime so you may want to be aggressive in paying them off.

NEGOTIATING BROKER FEES

We have negotiated the purchase price down by splitting the broker's fees with the seller. We did this because we had enough positive cash flow coming from the new property to pay the broker in the form of a note. Utilizing only one broker for both sides enabled us to gain a lower purchase price. Below is the actual example:

Purchase Price - $4,075,000 (down $62,125 because of note from broker)

Broker's Fee – 3% or $126,000

Split Fee - $61,125.00 paid in the form of a note over 10 years at 5% to the brokers company.

This may not be ideal for most negotiations, but our group had a strike price that we needed hit and this helped us get there.

We have also negotiated a reduction in the percentage the broker was getting in commission in order to get the seller to drop his price. This was utilizing one broker between both parties. Our example is below.

Example
Purchase Price - $4,200,000

Broker's Fee - 4% or $168,000

Broker Fee Reduction – brought down by 1% or $42,000

New Purchase Price - $4,158,000

This was a long and challenging negotiation so everyone had to give a little to make this deal work.

We try to use one broker per deal to represent seller and buyer. We realize some investors would not recommend this, but our experience has shown that a single broker acts as a peacemaker to bring both sides together. Utilizing one broker also allows that single broker to take the entire commission, which means they are more invested in the deal going through, and will do everything in their power to close even if it means taking a smaller commission.

SELLER REPAIRS PRIOR TO CLOSING

Usually, sellers are oblivious to the real issues of the property and believe you are simply trying to pocket a few extra bucks when discussing a repair allowance. The easiest way around this is to have them to make the repairs the property under your supervision. Your objective is to get the deferred maintenance repaired; you don't care if they pay for it or pay you to do it. It just needs to get done.
We have had success with sellers fixing their deferred maintenance a month prior to closing.

It pays to ask. We recently received over $20,000 in windows from a mom-and-pop owner because the current windows were foggy and near the end of their usefulness.

The great thing about these seller repairs is that it enables your staff to focus on other projects. Because money isn't changing hands, we have found that this can be a very profitable part of the closing process. For some reason it's harder to get an owner to give your $20,000 then it is for him to pay $20,000 for windows. Don't ask me why, but we have seen it time and time again.

REPAIR ALLOWANCE

The repair allowance is money to be transferred from the seller to the buyer (you) at closing. Remember, this is all negotiable so make sure that if you are asking for $8,000 to renovate a gutted unit, you have a way of showing why it's going to cost $8,000. Any non-operable part of the apartment complex is in play when it comes to repair allowances. It all depends on how motivated your seller is and how well you broker can present your case.

Glossary

Percent Down or Down Payment

This will be a cash payment put up by you or your group of investors. We typically put down 10%-15% of the purchase price when buying mom-and-pop apartments as a down payment. This strategy allows for higher cash on cash returns and requires less capital to get the deal done. (Side note– how amazing is it that you can put say 15% into a property worth $1,000,000 and take full control of the asset while your tenants pay your remaining balance.) This will only work if you buy right, manage right, and finance right.

Maturity Date

The maturity date refers to the lifespan of the loan. A loan that has a long life span and eventually reduces to zero is called a fully amortizing loan. The maturity period of this type of loan is always the length of the amortization. Conversely, a loan that ends abruptly is called a "term" loan. These types of loans are more common with multifamily properties, and the length of the loan can vary from one to fifteen years. Once the loan comes due at the end of the term, a large payment called a balloon payment is required. Term loans are not self-amortizing. Calculating principal and interest is identical for both types of loans, the only difference is the maturity date. If you can't come up with the balloon payment for the term loan, then we recommend refinancing the loan.

Amortization

Amortization is the distribution of payments over a period of time. It differs from other repayment schedules, in that each payment has a portion of the interest and the principal, eventually reducing to zero.

For our use, we are looking at the interest on the declining principle and the number of years on the loan. The longer the amortization, the greater your annual cash flow. Most community banks will only offer up to twenty years of amortization but we have usually found some willing to go to 25 years. This is an area that we have found banks to be very willing to negotiate on. We have seen the difference in our annual cash-on-cash go from 11.7% when calculating a 20-year amortization to 19.1% when calculating a 25-year amortization while forecasting for a potential acquisition.

Essentially, if you can go from a 20-year to a 25-year loan, your monthly income will increase because your payments are lower. The more you can rely on other people's money, the better.

Our actual example looked like this:

25-year amortization at 5% interest rate = 19.1% cash on cash return

20-year amortization at 5% interest rate = 11.7% cash on cash return

This can have a huge impact on your yearly cash flow. Remember though, this is all dependent on your personal investment strategies and goals. Pushing the amortization schedule out five more years will keep you five more years away from the remaining equity in the property.

BALLOON PAYMENTS

Balloon loans are not fully amortizing and terms will need to be renegotiated after the set term, which is typically, but not always, five years. With a balloon loan, you could buy and manage right, but within five years your interest rate could jump five points and dry up your cash flow. Remember, interest rates fluctuate with the market, and could have gone up since you bought the property. This is why the ultimate goal is to reposition the property and then refinance the loan to an FHA type product that is fully amortizing with a fixed interest rate. All of the secondary market lenders will require strong occupancy, which makes the repositioning piece so important.

LOAN TO VALUE

Loan to Value is a ratio used to describe the amount of your loan to the value of the property being purchased. You may hear the bankers refer to this as LTV. We typically request an 85% loan to value. This just means that the loan is 85% of the value, or sales price. If the property cost $1,000,000, the loan would be $850,000.

INTEREST RATES

Interest rates are the amount charged by a lender to a borrower for the use of an asset. We like to think of interest as a rental charge to the borrower for using the asset. Real estate owners benefit when rates go up and down. If rates go down, then the owner can refinance the property. If rates go up due to inflation, your rents will increase and you will be paying your loan off with cheaper dollars.

INTEREST-ONLY PAYMENTS

You can request that the first six months to one year of your loan are interest-only payments, instead of principal plus interest. If you choose this route, you will pay less on your monthly payments initially. You can request this from banks that you've been doing business with for a while. If you don't have a relationship, it might be difficult to negotiate an arrangement like this. We have found that clearly articulating your strategy and business plan to the potential lender will help the bank see why it's in their best interest to make this concession.

GUARANTORS

This is the guarantee that the bank will ask for when negotiating a loan. Typically, community and local banks will ask all investors to guarantee up to 100% of the loan amount. Therefore, if the property forecloses, each investor will handle the outstanding debt after the foreclosure sells. Guarantors give the bank more security because if one of the investors becomes bankrupt, they can go to the remaining investors for 100% of the outstanding debt. It's important to note, however, that this can be negotiated.

If you guarantee 100% of the loan, you will have an unbalanced personal balance sheet. You may only own only 35% of the property but they bank will be asking you to guarantee 100%. You should only attempt to guarantee your individual ownership in the investment by telling the bank that you would like "pro-rata" guarantees.

A NOTE ABOUT FEES

As we were writing this section, Jake was kicking himself because he was on the phone with a bank literally the day before and asked the banker "Since we are borrowing $3,460,000 don't you think a 1% origination fee is a bit steep? Can't we knock it down a tick? Say .75%?"

The loan officer immediately said "Sure, no problem." That might seem great at first, but Jake felt sick to his stomach. The broker had responded so quickly that Jake knew he definitely had more room to go down. Please learn from this mistake to save yourself money in the future! Either:

1. Ask them how low they are willing to go and then ask for a reduction in the number they present you. Putting the ball in their court gives you a good idea of what they think is fair.

2. Start lower than three-fourths (75%) of the original offer.

Prepayment Penalty

Let's say your balloon payment is fixed for five years, and at year three you take your loan to another lender. They will charge a fee because you broke the contract before those five years were up. This prepayment penalty is usually calculated as a percentage of the total loan.

We have run into the 3-2-1 penalty most often. It's usually defined as follows:

3% - penalty within the first twelve months of the loan

2% - penalty within the second twelve months of the loan

1% - penalty within the third twelve months of the loan

Remember, this isn't a hard and fast rule for balloon loans. Make sure you understand the prepayment penalty terms that you agree to when you take out a loan.

Deed

A deed is any legal instrument in writing that passes, affirms, or confirms an interest, right, or property. It must be signed, attested, delivered, and in some jurisdictions sealed. It is commonly associated with transferring the title of the property.

The grantor of a deed (seller) is conveying ownership to the grantee (buyer). There are a few types of deeds: quitclaim, special warranty, deed of trust.

A quitclaim deed makes no warranties as to the ownership of the property but only transfers interest to the grantee. A quitclaim deed does not contain any title covenant. The grantor transfers whatever interest he possesses at the time the transfer occurs. This type of deed is most commonly used in a divorce where one spouse transfers their interest to the ex-spouse.

A special warranty deed is a deed whereby the seller conveys title to the buyer and promises that he has clear ownership of the property. The grantor is promising that he has done nothing during his ownership to affect title of the property once it has been conveyed to the buyer.

A deed of trust is similar to a mortgage. The borrower transfers title of the property to a trustee, who holds the property in trust as security for repaying the debt. Once the borrower repays the debt, the ownership is released to the borrower and the trustee's ownership is terminated. If the borrower fails to repay the loan, the trustee has the right to sell the property and recoup their losses. Several states employ the deed of trust, such as California, as an alternative to a mortgage. As you can see, banks prefer this instrument because it is much easier to repossess a property from default and sell it to recoup any losses.

FORMS OF OWNERSHIP

Real Estate can be held in several forms of ownership. These forms include Individual Ownership, Joint Tenancy, Tenancy in Common, Partnerships, Limited Liability Company, Corporation, and Trusts. The only ownership entity that we would recommend to investors is the Limited Liability Company. The LLC, as it is commonly referred to, is a hybrid entity that incorporates elements of partnerships and corporations. It is an entity that provides limited liability to its "members" and allows for pass-through income taxation. It is a fairly simple entity to create, and we form a new LLC for each property to take advantage of the liability protection that it delivers. If one property is being sued, this will not affect the other properties because they are being held by different LLCs. It will cost you more in accounting fees to have your properties in separate LLCs, but the protection far exceeds the professional fees.

Operating and managing an LLC is similar to a corporation. Owners are referred to as members, and the LLC files articles of organization instead of articles of incorporation. You will have to create an operating agreement to be able to run the LLC. Owners of the LLC are listed either as managing members or general members.

Unfortunately, banks will still require you to personally guarantee repayment of the loan if it is a recourse loan. Remember, everything is negotiable, including the percent that you guarantee. It is imperative that you consult with your legal team as to the entity you should choose to hold you real estate.

CHAPTER 9 SUMMARY

Finance Right

1. Bridge loan with local bank.

2. Reposition property within 3 years.

3. Refinance to a non-recourse loan.

Time for action

1. What relationships have you established with the local bankers?

2. Have you prepared an investment book to share you story with the banks?

3. Are you ready to begin your journey in multifamily investing?

Get ready...the ride is about to start.

Check out www.jakeandgino.com for more wealth building tips

CHAPTER 10

THE RICHEST MAN IN MULTIFAMILY
AND CASE STUDIES

The Richest Man in Babylon, written by George Clason, is a must read for all investors. Below are the "Seven Cures for a Lean Purse" according to the protagonist, Arked. We will be going through them one by one, illustrating how real estate can be your remedy.

1. START THY PURSE TO FATTENING

Arkad, the richest man in Babylon, begins by telling his audience to save one coin out of every ten that is earned. This is wise financial advice. You will learn how to delay instant gratification and begin to budget your saving and spending, two key components in any real estate investment. Saving money will also give you the momentum to continue investing. We equate this to setting up your initial capital investment account. Saving 10% of your earnings to reinvest is a great way to get started, but if you can manage it, save more. This will be used as seed money for your first investment.

2. CONTROL THY EXPENDITURES

This is much easier said than done. It is vital to control spending after you have completed your first deal, especially when repositioning an apartment. For instance, a "fool" would install granite countertops in a C property. Luxury items don't add any real value to the property; cheaper Formica countertops would have served the identical purpose for a fraction of the cost. This "fool" will soon part ways with his investment.

This principle also carries over to our personal lives. It doesn't matter how much a person earns, but how you keep. When a person gets a raise, he might buy a car or a bigger house on impulse, instead of looking to the future. An impulsive buyer will always end up struggling. Your budget will allow you to control and monitor spending, while highlighting any weaknesses in your income statement. A budget will also give you the discipline to save 10% of your earnings.

3. MAKE THY GOLD MULTIPLY

Now that saving 10% is part of your routine, the next task is to put your savings to work. Your wealth will never explode unless you learn to invest savings and allow them to multiply. This is the stage where you will reinvest your profits into more multifamily investments. Einstein said it best: "The strongest force on earth is compound interest." Real estate is one of the best investments for multiplying your treasure. Cash flow can also provide for living expenses, and the increased value and equity you build up will lead to the continued growth of your wealth.

4. GUARD THY TREASURES FROM LOSS

Before you invest in any instrument, whether stocks, bonds or real estate, it is imperative that you seek out a mentor and begin to learn as much as possible about that investment. Their knowledge will help you to guard against losing your capital.

In the book, Arkad explains how he lost his first investment by lending money to a brick-maker to purchase jewels. When the brick-maker returned, he came with bits of glass instead. Real estate is an excellent vehicle to guard your treasures because you are in control of the investment. However, if you neglect your due diligence, you might be losing money every month. The broker or seller might mislead you, leaving you with something of no value.

Because you're in charge, you can do the research yourself and make the right decision. You're not leaving your investment up to a hedge fund manager. There is no CEO running a company, and no worries about third-quarter profits coming in below expectations. No middleman, or "brick-maker" to get in your way. It's only you and your partner controlling the property and all the major decisions.

There are various ways to guard your treasures in real estate. All investors have to purchase insurance on the property in case of damage. Most savvy investors make sure to include business interruption insurance, additional umbrella liability insurance, and other coverages that your insurance agent will recommend. We sign operating agreements with the partners to detail our relationship and how the partnership is to function. We also set up LLC's to protect us from any liability that may occur on the property. The LLC would be held liable, but none of the partners would be held personally liable.

5. MAKE OF THY DWELLING A PROFITABLE INVESTMENT

Some investors start out by buying smaller units and occupy one of the apartments while collecting rent on the other units. This is an excellent strategy to create wealth and lower expenses. Your tenants are paying the mortgage and expenses while you are living rent-free. A great way to start is with a duplex. This will allow you to invest more of your earned income into new investments, instead of living expenses.

6. INSURE A FUTURE INCOME

Most people in our society are counting on Social Security for their retirement needs. At age 65, 1% of the population will be considered wealthy, 4% will have enough money set aside for retirement, 3% will still be employed, a whopping 63% will be dependent on Social Security (or some charity) and 29% will be deceased. Growing old is inevitable, but we all have the choice of where we end up.

There is no other vehicle that provides for retirement better than real estate. If you have held the property for years, you can either sell the property or continue to hold it for cash flow. If you decide to sell, then you can take back a mortgage and receive monthly payments. Several investments offer future monthly payments, but real estate has added tax advantages. If selling is not part of your DNA, then continue to hold the property and hire a management company to run it when you retire.

Refinancing a property is another strategy for ensuring a future income. If a property has been owned for many years, the equity has been built up and the owner can opt to pull out some of that equity. The beauty of this option is that the money refinanced from the property is tax-free. Most owners who are advanced in age usually have fewer write-offs and tend to incur a larger tax bill. By refinancing, the owner will incur no added tax liability and will keep all of his money (the old adage, it's what you keep that counts).

7. INCREASE THY ABILITY TO EARN

Never stop learning your craft. There are countless property types in real estate, such as self-storage, office, multifamily, single family, and medical. There are just as many strategies: rent to own, master lease, buy and hold, buy and flip, and wholesaling, just to name a few. Investors should always continue to educate themselves because the market is constantly changing, and while one strategy may be working, the next market cycle could render that strategy obsolete. Our main focus is to buy and hold multifamily apartments, but we still familiarize ourselves with all the other strategies. It is a well known fact that the buy and hold strategy is a great strategy for serious wealth building. Much of the "old money" in the U.S. has been amassed through property ownership.

CONCLUSION

The window for purchasing these mom-and-pop type apartments is shrinking. Real estate firms are growing in size, and trusts buy up more and more properties each year. As we have outlined, the best opportunity to grow your wealth is buying from mom-and-pop owners. Time is of the essence. The sooner you set up an investment crew the better chance you have of building your legacy.

If you remain persistent and follow our framework, you will eventually succeed. We hope at this point you realize that just about everything in real estate is negotiable. Bottom line, don't give up. Many times we're tempted to give in to a seller or a bank, but it's important to be a disciplined investor and to stick to your guns.

Follow the framework:

Buy Right

Manage Right

Finance Right

The necessary info is all here, and it's time to follow the yellow brick road to your financial independence. If you would like to benefit from the direct accountability and teaching that comes with our coaching program, go to our website, www.jakeandgino.com, and click on the coaching tab for more info. We also offer deal analyzer software to simplify your deal analysis. All you have to do is plug in the numbers and roll with it.

CASE STUDY 1: COURTYARD COTTAGES

Courtyard Cottages is a 25-unit multifamily property consisting of efficiency apartments, one-bedroom cottages, 4-plex buildings, and duplex houses.

OBSTACLES:

- Weekly paying tenants that led to transient tenant base

- Drug problems

- Majority of payments made in cash

- Units were furnished which resulted in bed bugs

- Interior and exterior deferred maintenance

- No tenant screening process

- Property Rules and Regulations were not enforced

- Unsafe environment for tenants

- Terrible image and reputation

SOLUTION:

By implementing systems for screening tenants and collecting rent, we were able to change the culture of the property. All renters were charged an application fee and were put through background and criminal checks. Tenants who were not paying were evicted. The same people not paying rent were the ones involved with drugs, so when they were evicted the criminal problem solved itself.

We then changed over to monthly leasing and created a more stable tenant base. Tenants were required to pay by check or money order. This led to a more stable monthly rental income and reduced maintenance expenses. A manager was hired for the property which increased resident retention as well as tenant satisfaction.

Exterior maintenance commenced immediately to attract higher quality renters. Buildings were power washed and painted, landscaping was planted, and debris was removed throughout the property. The interior furniture was sent to the dump and the infested units were heat treated for bed bugs. We cleared out three sheds on the property and began to rent them as storage. All vendors were required to re-submit quotes for new work, and three bids were secured for each job.

RESULTS:

- Quality of the tenant base rose dramatically, which led to increased revenue and tenant retention.

- Expenses were lowered due to lower tenant turnover.

- Safety of the community rose, and the neighborhood was transformed into what we call "Modern Affordability."

- The property reputation was changed. The mail lady has since thanked us because she is no longer scared to deliver the mail.

- The drug problems have been resolved.

- Based on an 8% cap rate, the property has appreciated $350,000.

- Our cash on cash return has averaged 34%.

- Gross annual income has increased $6,000.

Case Study 2: Hickory Hill Apartments

36-unit complex consisting of spacious one-bedroom apartments

Obstacles

- Interior and exterior deferred maintenance

- Poorly managed asset with low rents and low monthly rental income

- Resident manager cut deals with tenants and worked on the barter system

- High vacancy rate

- Expenses higher than normal

- Burnt out mom-and-pop owners

Solution:

We immediately began maintenance on the exterior of the property and the laundry facility. Coinmach was hired to assume responsibility of the laundry room and provided new machines at no additional cost to us. Units that were vacant were rehabbed and rented at a higher rate. Any units that became vacant were also rehabbed and re-rented at the higher price.

New vendors were hired to perform landscaping and garbage collection, which resulted in substantial savings. We were allowed to bundle these vendors with our other property, which led to further increased savings. A manager was hired and paid on performance at a rate of about 4% of gross rents.

RESULTS:

- Gross rental income increased from $10,800 per month to $18,000 per month, a 66% increase.

- Our new management system led to higher gross income and increased occupancy.

- A RUBS system was implemented to increase income

- Tenant base stabilized.

- Property went to full capacity.

- Rent for current tenants could be increased to market rent.

- Based on an 8% cap rate, the property has appreciated $590,000.

- Our cash on cash return has averaged 11%.

- Gross annual income has increased $86,400.

CASE STUDY 3: PARK PLACE APARTMENTS WEST AND SOUTH

136 unit multifamily apartment complex consisting of 88 two-bedroom units and 48 three-bedroom units.

OBSTACLES:

- Poorly managed asset that led to 30 out of 136 units left vacant (78 % occupied at time of acquisition)

- Six units being used as storage rooms

- Out of control expenses

- Rents that were 25% below market

- Owners paid all utilities

- No amenities on property

- Major deferred maintenance on exterior and interior

- No maintenance program

- Disgruntled tenants

- No web presence

- Disgruntled family ownership (family feud)

- Property taxes had not been paid

SOLUTION:

We saw the tremendous potential this property could offer to the right owners. We changed the name to Park Place Apartments and put "under new management" signs at all entrances. Our web team put together a great new website. This website was great for marketing and current tenant maintenance needs. Coinmach replaced all laundry machines and took over operations. A RUBS system was implemented which increased income dramatically.

Park Place is located next to a large manufacturing plant, which employs 4,500 workers. We established a good relationship with human resources so that we would become the most favored apartment complex in the area. In just ten weeks after our acquisition, all thirty vacant apartments were filled.

We instituted a maintenance program and hired two techs to tackle all outstanding maintenance issues. This led to a higher satisfaction from tenants and increased tenant retention. Tenants were thrilled to have needs met in a timely fashion.

RESULTS:

- Tenant satisfaction has soared, leading to increased rent and tenant retention.

- Gross rental income increased from $54,000 per month to $84,000 per month within nine months, a 60% increase. This is an increase of $360,000 per year.

- Occupancy has been increased to 96% +.

- Based on an 8% cap rate, the property has appreciated $3,425,000.

- Gross annual income has increased $360,000.

- The refinance allowed us to pull out $1,600,000+ in equity.

Case Study 4: Park Place Apartments North

24 Unit apartment complex consisting 23 two-bedroom and 1 one-bed-room apartments.

Obstacles

- Interior and exterior deferred maintenance

- Poorly managed property that was neglected

- Resident manager cut deals with tenants and worked on the barter system

- Expenses higher than normal

- Out of town owner

Solution:

We immediately began maintenance on the exterior of the property as well as the laundry facility. Coinmach was hired to assume responsibility of laundry room and provided new machines at no additional cost. Units that were vacant were rehabbed and rented at market rates. Any units that became vacant were also rehabbed and re-rented at the higher price. Our vendors were contacted to perform landscaping and garbage collection that resulted in substantial savings. Our management company was put in place to reposition the property.

RESULTS:

- Gross rental income increased from $10,500 per month to $13,200 per month.

- Our new management system led to increased occupancy.

- A RUBS system lead to additional revenue.

- Tenant base stabilized.

- Value was added to the property by managing effectively with good customer service.

- Property is fully rented, even though several tenants with previous leases are currently on the property with lower than market rent. Once tenants vacate apartments, units will be rehabbed and rent will be raised to current rate.

- Based on an 8% cap rate, the property has appreciated $125,000.

- Gross annual income has increased by $36,000.

Case Study 5: Jefferson City Portfolio

Micro Re-positioning

281-unit multifamily property comprised of studio, one, and two-bedroom apartments, along with two, three, and four-bedroom town homes.

Obstacles

- Mom and Pop apartment with high expenses and high labor costs

- High expenses for landscaping, management, payroll and phone service

- Rents were below market

- Extremely high utility expense

- No Ratio Utility Billing System (RUBS)

- Unattractive website and poor marketing

Purchase:

- $11,000,000 purchase price.

- Bought at an 8% Cap Rate

- 80% bank financing

  o 4.25% interest rate

  o 25-year amortization

  o 5-year term

- 20% owner financing
  - ○ 4.5% interest rate
  - ○ 30-year amortization
  - ○ 5-year balloon

We purchased this 281- unit multifamily property with **no** money down! This was only possible because we had a terrific relationship with the local bank.

SOLUTIONS:

We assumed management and began to implement the Wheelbarrow Profits repositioning framework. All tenants who were not on a lease were brought up to market rent and charged a RUBS fee. We hired a full time leasing agent and maintained three maintenance workers full time. All new rental units were raised to market rent.

RESULTS:

- At the time of this writing we just closed on this deal. Check out www.jakeandgino.com for updates.

Financial Timeline of Park Place

Financing a new investment can be tough, and it takes a lot of determination to pull it off. Deals never go through without a few bumps in the road. Below is a timeline of one of our more recent deals, for our Park Place property.

August 2014

- Met broker to discuss financing options
- Began to discuss rates, terms, bank lenders

October 2014

- Introduced to first lender
- Terms Offered: 200 basis points above 10-year treasury
- 10-year balloon
- 30-year amortization
- 25% LTV
- Appraisal deposit: $10,000 (actual cost $4,000)

November 2014

- Ordered appraisal. Took one month from order to receive appraisal

December 2014

- Appraisal comes back at $5.7 million
- 75% LTV mortgage amount is $4.275 million

- We were expecting $6 million appraisal with $4.5 million mortgage
- This would leave us with $700,000 net proceeds after closing costs, and payment of notes.

MID-DECEMBER

- Deal is dead. Appraiser does not want to budge with valuation. He estimates expenses at $3,300 per unit, we are running at $2,800 per unit.
- Make contact with other lenders.
- Engage second lender.

JANUARY 2014

- Terms with second lender:
- 30-year amortization
- 220 basis points above 10-year treasury bond
- 25% LTV
- $40,000 down payment for closing costs
- Capped loan amount to $4.4 million
- Very detailed contract
- Contract expires in June 2015

FEBRUARY 2014

- Ordered appraisal.

March 2014

- Appraisal comes in at $6.5 Million. SUCCESS!!

- Hold on… Second lender questions valuation performed by its own appraiser.

April 2014

- Second lender drops valuation to $6.3 million and raises LTV to 30%.

Mid-April

- Renegotiate LTV back to 25%.

- Loan Amount: $4.725 Million

- Begin negotiating capital expenditure amount. The broker projects $250,000.

May 2015

- Order Engineering and Environmental Studies

- Second lender will not go above $4.4 million total loan amount or 25% loan to value.

- Looking at alternative financing.

June 2015

- Came to terms with lender that currently held the mortgage:

- $6.33 million appraisal

- 80% loan to value

- 25-year amortization

- 4.65 % interest rate

- $1,617,838 cash out amount

- $5,064,000 loan amount

After ten grueling months and lots of hard work, our patience and persistence has paid off!

Income Statement

Revenue

Gross Scheduled Rent   _____

Less: Vacancy   _____

Less: Concessions   _____

Equals Net Rental Income   _____

Plus: Other Income   _____

Equals: Total Income   _____

Operating Expenses:

Management   _____

Utilities   _____

Advertising and Marketing   _____

Property and Payroll taxes   _____

Insurance   _____

Payroll   _____

Repairs and Maintenance   _____

Professional fees (accountant, legal)   _____

Supplies   _____

Broker Commissions   _____

Travel expenses _____

Total Operating Expenses: _____

Revenue-Operating Expenses = Net Operating Income

Net Operating Income _____

Less: Capital Expenses _____

Less: Debt Service _____

Equals: Cash Flow _____

NOI less Depreciation plus Interest = Taxable Income

Wheelbarrow Profits   Broker Name

123 Main Street   Address

Any Town, USA

Dear Broker,

Wheelbarrow profits is currently investing in the Knoxville market purchasing underperforming, multifamily assets that are being run inefficiently and can be repositioned through rental income growth and reduction in expenses. We are targeting properties that are renting to blue collar workers. Visit our website **www.jakeandgino.com** to learn more about our investment strategy and view our credibility book that lists our current portfolio.

Our strategy is to:

1. Purchase the asset
2. Rebrand the asset by changing the name and changing signage
3. Perform all deferred maintenance, and create a safe, clean and hospitable environment for our tenants.
4. Reduce expenses by self-managing and achieving economies of scale with other properties
5. Raise rents to market rate
6. Refinance property

Our specific criteria:

Our strategy is to purchase B and C properties that have the potential for adding value through raising rents and streamlining operations and are located next to manufacturing and retail locations. We are looking for properties that contain:

- Between 50 to 150 units

- East Tennessee

- 10% cash on cash return and at least an 8 cap rate

- Unit mix predominantly 2 bedrooms, with at least two, 2 bedroom units for each one 1 bedroom unit

- Ability to institute Ratio Utility Billback System (RUBS)

- Deferred maintenance existing on the property

- Below market rents

- Vacancy rate higher than market average

- Located next to shopping and employment

- High expenses

If you have any properties that meet these specifications, please contact us. We are looking forward to working with you.

Sincerely,

Made in the USA
Coppell, TX
23 January 2020

14911412R00095